THE ROYAL COURT THEATRE PRESENTS

Goats

by Liwaa Yazji
Translated by Katharine Halls

Goats was first performed at the Royal Court Jerwood Theatre Downstairs, Sloane Square, on Friday 24 November 2017.

Goats is presented as part of International Playwrights: A Genesis Foundation Project.

Goats is also supported by the British Council.

Goats

by Liwaa Yazji
Translated by Katharine Halls

CAST (in alphabetical order)

Jude **Ali Barouti**
Imm Nabil **Ishia Bennison**
Abu Firas **Carlos Chahine**
Adnan **Amir El-Masry**
Imm Ghassan **Souad Faress**
Abu al-Tayyib **Amer Hlehel**
Mudar **Ethan Kai**
Abu Karim **Khalid Laith**
Fadi **Adnan Mustafa**
Zahra **Isabella Nefar**
Sami **Farshid Rokey**
The Presenter/Imm al-Tayyib **Sirine Saba**

All other parts are played by members of the company:

Abu Lu'ay, Imm Mazen, Imm Aziz, Abu Ala' and Imm Ala', Abu Jamal
and Imm Jamal, Imm Marwan, Sheikh Abu Salam, Abu Ahmad, Abu
Muhammad 1, Abu Muhammad 2, Abu al-Reem, Abu Samer and Imm
Samer, Imm Salma, Abu Rami and Imm Rami, and Imm Nader.

Goats

by Liwaa Yazji
Translated by Katharine Halls

Director **Hamish Pirie**
Designer **Rosie Elnile**
Video Designer **Ian William Galloway**
Lighting Designer **Muaz Aljubeh**
Music Consultants **Mark Gergis, Rizan Said**
Sound Designer **Tom Gibbons**
Movement Director **Quang Kien Van**
Associate Translator **Yasmine Seale**
Assistant Director **Nimmo Ismail**
Assistant Sound Designer **Grzegorz Staniewicz**
Vocal Coach **Hugh O'Shea**
Fight Director **Bret Yount**
Casting Director **Amy Ball**
Production Manager **Marius Rønning**
Costume Supervisor **Lucy Walshaw**
International Director **Elyse Dodgson**
Associate Director (International) **Sam Pritchard**
International Assistant **Sarah Murray**
Stage Manager **Alex Constantin**
Deputy Stage Manager **Emma Tooze**
Assistant Stage Manager **Sayeedah Supersad**
Stage Management Work Placement **Izzy Evans**
Set Built by **Ridiculous Solutions**

The Royal Court would like to thank the following for their help with this production:

The team at Animal Actors, Harold Addo, Nadia Albina, Brian Bovell, Jenny Grand, Grace Gummer, Amar Haj Ahmad, Baraa Halabieh, Michael Karim, Ismail Kaseem, Shaza Khandakji, Ahmed Najar, Jonjo O'Neill, Ammar Raed, Charif Sada, Abd Alrahman Salama, Aso Sherabayani, Terry's Discount Store, Eckhard Thiemann, Badria Timimi, Alan Williams.

Goats has been generously supported by the following individuals:

G & O Al-Qattan, Wendy Fisher, Anatol Orient, Bissar Sleiman, Maria Sukkar, Mahdi Yahya and those who wish to remain anonymous.

The animals which appear in this production are expertly cared for by a team of certified trainers who ensure their welfare is safeguarded at all times. The producers have worked with the handlers and professional animal welfare bodies to ensure the highest standards of wellbeing for the animals.

Goats

by Liwaa Yazji

Translated by Katharine Halls

Liwaa Yazji (Writer)

For the Royal Court: **Goats (Told from the Inside reading).**

Other theatre includes: **Here in the Park, Q&Q (Birth Festival, Royal Exchange, Manchester/ Edinburgh International Festival).**

Television includes: **The Brothers, Heim.**

Films include: **Haunted (feature documentary).**

Awards include: **Special Mention in the First Film Competition at FID Marseille, GIGAF Festival Tunis Al-Waha Bronze Award (Haunted).**

Liwaa Yazji is a Syrian playwright, filmmaker, screenwriter and poet. She was born in Moscow and grew up in Damascus. She has published a volume of poetry In Peace, We Leave Home, and was resident poet at Poets House New York in 2015 where her book, Three Poems, was published in English. Liwaa took part in the Royal Court workshops in Beirut with writers from Lebanon and Syria from 2014–15 where she began the work on Goats, supported by the British Council.

Muaz Aljubeh (Lighting Designer)

Theatre includes: **Taha (Young Vic); Azza (Shiberhur Theatre Company, Palestine); Where Can I Find Someone like You, Ali? (International tour); Racheman (Tokyo Art International Festival), Smile – You are Palestinian, Alive from Palestine - Stories Under Occupation (& International tour), Al-Zeir Salem (Al-Kasaba Theatre and Cinematheque).**

Dance includes: **Against a Hard Surface (Yaa Samar! Dance Theatre), 100% Water (Nawal Iskandarani), Sahet Elward, At the Checkpoint (Sareyyet Ramallah).**

Live music shows include: **Mina (Terez Sliman), Hajess (Sanaa Moussa), Asfar (Trio Jubran).**

Muaz is a Jerusalem-based Palestinian lighting designer who has toured productions nationally and internationally since 1995. He was the technical director for Al-Kasaba Theatre and Cinematheque for almost 20 years and has been the technical director for the Ramallah Contemporary Dance Festival since its founding in 2006.

Ali Barouti (Jude)

Television includes: **Tyrant.**

Film includes: **Patrick, Daytimer.**

Goats is Ali's professional stage debut.

Ishia Bennison (Imm Nabil)

For the Royal Court: **Our Private Life.**

Other theatre includes: **Half Life (Theatre Royal, Bath); Candide, A Mad World My Masters (& UK tour), A New Way to Please You, Sejanus: His Fall, Speaking Like Magpies, Cymbeline, Measure for Measure (RSC); Julius Caesar (Donmar); The Importance of Being Earnest (Rose, Kingston/Hong Kong Festival); The Canterbury Tales (Rose, Kingston/Tour); A Couple of Poor, Polish Speaking Romanians (Soho); Bites (Bush); Strange Orchestra, Mother Courage (Orange Tree); Who's Afraid of Virginia Woolf? (Manchester Library); Arabian Nights (Young Vic); Antony & Cleopatra (BAM, NYC); A Midsummer Night's Dream, The Merry Wives, Romeo & Juliet (Northern Broadsides); Richard III (Riverside Studios/Tower of London); Medea (Lilian Baylis); Les Misérables (Nottingham Playhouse); Turcaret (Gate); One for the Road (tour); Educating Rita (Oxford Playhouse).**

Television includes: **Happy Valley, Last Tango in Halifax, True Dare Kiss, At Home With The Braithwaites, Holby City, Emmerdale, Coronation Street, Burnside, Love Hurts, Give & Take, The Storyteller, Bread, EastEnders, Much Ado About Nothing, Mitch: A Family Affair, Kessler, Bid For Power, King David, Anno Domini, The Awakening, Jesus Of Nazareth.**

Carlos Chahine (Abu Firas)

Theatre includes: **The Cherry Orchard (Al Madina, Beirut); The Three Sisters (Limoges); The Tempest (Créteil); Macbeth (Cifas, Belgium); Scratching on Things I Could Disavow: A History of Art in the Arab World (Festival d'automne, Paris); The Suicide, The Golem (Athénée, Paris); À la Renverse (Athevains, Paris); The Inspector General, La Remise, Iphigénie Hotel, La Dame de chez Maxim (Amandiers, Nanterre); Phaedra (La Tempête, Paris); Le Misanthrope (Nimes); The Changelling, Cent Millions qui Tombent (Gennevilliers); Chronique des Jours Souverains (Caen); Minna Von Barnhelm (Le Maillon, Strasbourg); À la Conquête du Pôle Sud, Joe Bousquet Rue de Verdun (Avignon Festival); Don Quichotte (Batie Festival, Geneva); Œdipe a Colone (Theatro Due Parma).**

Television includes: **Les Baisers de Secours, Escapade, Avocats et Associés, Carlos, Le Tableau Noir.**

Film includes: **The Insult, The Valley, Carlos, The Last Man, Terra Incognita, Le Vertige de la Feuille Blanche.**

Awards include: **Best Actor Singapore International Film Festival (The Last Man); Best Film Tribeca Film Festival, Best Film Dubai International Film Festival, Best Film Open Film Festival St Petersbourg, Best Film International Arab Film Festival Spain, Best Film Saint Paul les Trois Châteaux, Cinécinécourt Award Montpellier Film Festival (The North Road).**

Amir El-Masry (Adnan)

Television Includes: **The State, The Night Manager, McMafia, Ride Upon the Storm, Tyrant, Rude Boys.**

Films include: **Lost in London, Shoot, Rosewater, Ramadan Mabrouk Abu El Alamein Hamouda, El Thalatha Yeshtaghlonha.**

Awards Include: **Egyptian Oscar Award for Best Young Actor (Ramadan Mabrouk Abu El Alamein Hamouda).**

Goats is Amir's professional stage debut.

Rosie Elnile (Designer)

For the Royal Court: **Primetime 2017.**

Other theatre includes: **Unknown Island, The Convert (Gate); BIG GUNS (Yard); Hard C*ck (Spill festival); Loaded (Jacksons Lane).**

Rosie was the first Resident Design Assistant at the Donmar Warehouse from 2015–16.

Souad Faress (Imm Ghassan)

For the Royal Court: **The Great Celestial Cow, Minor Complications, Mahua (rehearsed reading), A Curse.**

Other theatre includes: **Winter Hill (Octagon, Bolton); Tiger Country, Sugar & Snow (Hampstead); Homebody/Kabul (Cheek by Jowl/ Young Vic); Celestina (Birmingham Rep); The House of Bernada Alba (Almeida); Small Miracle (Mercury, Colchester); The Permanent Way (Out of Joint/National).**

Television includes: **Game of Thrones, Apple Tree House, Brief Encounters, Berlin Station, Sense8, Cabbage & Patch, Vera, Doctors, Making of a Lady, Utopia, Hunted, Hollyoaks, The Sarah Jane Adventures, Silent Witness, Holby City, Law & Order, The Bill, Trial & Retribution, Casualty, Family Affairs, Being April, Coronation Street.**

Film includes: **Bridget Jones's Baby, Sixth Happiness, My Beautiful Laundrette, Bhaji on the Beach.**

Radio includes: **The Archers, Phonophone, Signal to Noise, Uma & the Fairy Queen, The 39 Steps, Earthsea, Zaatari, The Iran Season.**

Ian William Galloway
(Video Designer)

Theatre includes: **Mosquitoes (National); Singin' in The Rain, Gypsy, Elf: The Musical (West End); Schikaneder (Raimund, Vienna); Wendy & Peter Pan, The Gods Weep (RSC); The Absence of War, Spring Awakening, A Midsummer Night's Dream (Headlong); Oh! What a Lovely War (Theatre Royal, Stratford East); Beautiful Burnout, Lovesong (Frantic Assembly); Macbeth, The Missing (National Theatre of Scotland), Amadeus (Chichester Festival); The Graduate, Enjoy (West Yorkshire Playhouse); The Radicalisation of Bradley Manning, Mother Courage & her Children (National Theatre Wales); Hapgood (Hampstead); Est–ce Que Tu Dors? (Festival d'Avignon/Complicite); The Tempest, The Lion in Winter (Theatre Royal, Haymarket).**

Opera includes: **La Fanciulla Del West (La Scala); Madame Butterfly (Glyndebourne); Hansel & Gretel (Opera North); Agrippina (Theatre an der Wien); Eugene Onegin (& Metropolitan Opera), The Marriage of Figaro (ENO); Faust (Mariinsky); The Flying Dutchman (Scottish Opera); Juliette, Where the Wild Things Are (Bremer Oper); The Lion's Face, Seven Angels (The Opera Group); Hotel de Pekin (Nationale Reisopera); Sancta Susanna, Von Heute Auf Morgen (Opera de Lyon).**

Mark Gergis (Music Consultant)

As sound designer, film includes: **Oulaya's Wedding.**

As composer & sound designer, dance includes: **Dance Elixir (international tour).**

As producer, radio includes: **Flimsy Tomb, Radio Boredcast.**

Mark is a composer, producer and audio- visual archivist. He operates as a freelance producer, specializing in post-production, mastering, restoration, and sound design for film, exhibits, music and dialog editing. Mark has shared decades worth of archived international music with US-based record label Sublime Frequencies and his own label Sham Palace. His acclaimed two-hour audio- documentary I Remember Syria (2003) was re- issued in 2015, with all proceeds going toward Syrian relief charities.

Tom Gibbons (Sound Designer)

For the Royal Court: **Love Love Love.**

Other theatre includes: **The Lorax (Old Vic); Venus In Fur (Theatre Royal, Haymarket); Hamlet (Almeida/West End); Oresteia (Almeida/Trafalgar Studios); Mr Burns, 1984 (Almeida/West End/Broadway); A View from the Bridge (& West End), Life of Galileo, Happy Days, A Season in the Congo, Disco Pigs (Young Vic); Hedda Gabler, Sunset at the Villa Thalia, The Red Barn, People, Places & Things (National/West End); Les Misérables (Wermland Opera, Sweden); The Crucible (Broadway); Anna Karenina (Royal Exchange, Manchester); The Moderate Soprano, Elephants (Hampstead); White Devil, As You Like It (RSC); Translations, Plenty (Crucible, Sheffield); The Absence of War, Romeo & Juliet (Headlong); Lion Boy (Complicite); Henry IV, Julius Caesar (Donmar/St Ann's, Brooklyn); Grounded (Gate); The Spire (Salisbury Playhouse); The Sound of Heavy Rain, The Initiate, Our Teacher's a Troll, Lungs, London, The Angry Brigade, Wasted (Paines Plough); The Rover (Hampton Court Palace); Dead Heavy Fantastic (Liverpool Everyman); Chalet Lines, The Knowledge, Little Platoons, Fifty Ways to Leave Your Lover (Bush).**

Awards include: **Olivier Award for Best Sound Design (People, Places &Things).**

Katharine Halls (Translator)

For the Royal Court: **Ghalia's Miles (Told from the Inside reading/Edinburgh International Festival).**

Other theatre includes: **Aleppo: A Portrait of Absence – selected texts (Haus der Kulturen der Welt, Berlin); Whims of Freedom (& Maxim Gorki, Berlin/LIFT), Zig Zig (SHISH/Kaaitheater, Brussels).**

Film includes: **The Coming Attraction, The Vote, The Crossing, Out on the Street, Common State, Next to Paradise.**

Katharine studied Hebrew and Arabic at the University of Oxford and holds an MA in Arabic–English translation and interpreting. Her co-translation (with Adam Talib) of Raja Alem's The Dove's Necklace, winner of the International Prize for Arabic Fiction, appeared in 2016. Her translation for theatre includes work by Egyptian playwright Laila Soliman and independent Palestinian ensemble Khashabi Theatre.

Amer Hlehel (Abu al-Tayyib)

Theatre includes: **Taha (& Young Vic), Almushakhsati (Qadita); Lanterns of the King of Galilee (Palestinian National Theatre); Azza, In the Penal Colony, Bemazeed men alHuzn, I Am Yusuf & This is My Brother (& Young Vic), Atssi (Shiber Horr); The Tempest, The Comedy of Errors, Twelfth Night (RSC); Servant of Two Masters, Death & the Maiden, Hareq Al Ma'bad, What the Story is All About, The Barber of Baghdad (Al-Midan); Byn Harb Byn (Aysh); Diab (Masrahid Festival, Acre); A Day in Our Lives, The Mission (Acre Festival); The Baggage Packers (Haifa University); Darwish Ya Sayed (Masraheed Festival); Gilgamesh Didn't Die (Alhakawati Ensemble, Paris); The Order (Al-Niqab).**

Film includes: **Personal Affairs, The Idol, Man Without a Cell Phone, The Time That Remains, Amreeka, Paradise Now.**

Amer is the Artistic Director of the Al-Midan Theatre in Haifa.

Nimmo Ismail (Assistant Director)

As assistant director, theatre includes: **Wings (Young Vic); Quarter Life Crisis (Ovalhouse).**

As writer, theatre includes: **New Ways of Looking (Bush).**

Nimmo was a member of the Royal Court's Introduction to Playwriting group in 2016.

Ethan Kai (Mudar)

Television includes: **Emmerdale, Mount Pleasant, Doctors.**

Film includes: **Instrument of War.**

Goats is Ethan's professional stage debut.

Khalid Laith (Abu Karim)

Theatre includes: **Lawrence After Arabia (Hampstead); Tactical Questioning (Tricycle); Damascus (Traverse/59E59E, NYC); Shadow Language (503); Nameless (Cockpit); Leaving Home (King's Head/Blue Elephant).**

Television includes: **Deep State, Missing, Spooks, The Mark of Cain, Saddam's Tribe, The Bill, Occupation.**

Film includes: **American Assassin, A Hologram for the King, Killing Jesus, World War Z, Red 2, Djinn, Devil's Double.**

Adnan Mustafa (Fadi)

Film includes: **Yardie.**

Goats is Adnan's professional stage debut.

Isabella Nefar (Zahra)

Theatre includes: **Salomé (National); History of Qu, Borderline (Teatro Stehler); Sarabanda (Teatro Franco Parenti).**

Television includes: **Aspirin.**

Film includes: **Small City, Serenanta, This is Your Life.**

Hamish Pirie (Director)

For the Royal Court: **Primetime 2017, Human Animals, Violence & Son, Who Cares, Teh Internet is Serious Business.**

Other theatre includes: **Shibboleth (Abbey, Dublin); I'm With The Band (Traverse/Wales Millennium Centre); Quiz Show, Demos, 50 Plays for Edinburgh (Traverse); Love With a Capital 'L', 3 Seconds, Most Favoured, The Last Bloom (Traverse/Òran Mór); Bravo Figaro (Royal Opera House/Traverse); Salt Root & Roe (Donmar/Trafalgar Studios); Stacy (& Trafalgar Studios), Purgatory (Arcola); Pennies (nabokov); Paper House (Flight 5065).**

Hamish trained as Resident Assistant Director at Paines Plough and at the Donmar Warehouse. He was previously Associate Director at the Traverse Theatre. Hamish is an Associate Director at the Royal Court.

Farshid Rokey (Sami)

Theatre includes: **10,000 Smarties (Three Streets/ Oxford Old Fire Station); Another World (National); Martyr (Actors Touring Company); Love Your Soldiers (Crucible, Sheffield); Star Crossed (Bush); The Kite Runner (Nottingham Playhouse/Liverpool Playhouse); Mogadishu (Lyric, Hammersmith/ Royal Exchange, Manchester/UK tour); The Photographer (503); In the Unlikely Event of an Emergency (Soho).**

Television includes: **The Trial, Cuffs, Tyrant, Holby City, Our Girl, Family Tree, The Spa, Doctors, Freak, The Endz.**

Film includes: **Rise of the Foot Soldier II, Leave to Remain.**

Radio includes: **Stray, 4:30am, Flight, In Here, Islam People & Power, Crossing Continents, The Fanguler & the Twoof, The Listening Project, Welcome to Zaatari, The Boy from Aleppo who Painted the War, Mogadishu.**

Sirine Saba (The Presenter/Imm al-Tayyib)

For the Royal Court: **The Crossing Plays (& LIFT), Fireworks, The Spiral (Rough Cuts).**

Other theatre includes: **King Lear, Holy Warriors, Anthony & Cleopatra (Globe); Why It's Kicking Off Everywhere (Young Vic); The Intelligent Homosexual's Guide to Socialism & Capitalism (Hampstead); Another World, Nation, Sparkleshark (National); The Invisible (Bush); Next Fall (Southwark Playhouse); The Winter's Tale, A Midsummer Night's Dream, The Taming of the Shrew, Twelfth Night, HMS Pinafore (Regent's Park Open Air); The Fear of Breathing (Finborough); Scorched (Old Vic Tunnels); Testing The Echo (Out Of Joint/Tricycle); Baghdad Wedding (Soho); Beauty & the Beast, Midnight's Children (& Apollo, NYC); Pericles,**

The Tempest, The Winter's Tale, A Midsummer Night's Dream (& BAM, NYC), Tales From Ovid (& Young Vic), A Warwickshire Testimony (RSC); Cinderella (Bristol Old Vic); House & Garden (Royal & Derngate).

Television includes: **Clean Break, Why It's Kicking Off Everywhere, EastEnders, Unforgotten, Doctors, I Am Slave, Silent Witness, Footballer's Wives, The Bill, Prometheus.**

Film includes: **The Black Forest, Exhibition, Maestro, Death of the Revolution.**

Radio includes: **Borderland, World on the Move: First Born, Wide Sargasso Sea, The Listening Project, Welcome to Zaatari, Tumanbay, Trespasser's Guide to the Classics: 1001 Nights, Something Understood, Anthony & Cleopatra, From Fact to Fiction, The Brick, The Outsider, The Insider, The Reluctant Spy, The Deportation Room, In the Van, Marley Was Dead, My Daughter the Racist, The Smell of Fish, The Casper Loague Affair (Arabian Afternoons), A Dish of Pomegranates, The Porter & the Three Ladies, English in Afghanistan, The Locust & the Bird, Beirut Days, The Waves, The Invasion: Arab Chronicles of the First Crusade, The Night of the Mirage, Baghdad Wedding, Love & Loss.**

Rizan Said (Music Consultant)

As composer, songs include: **Bas Asma Mni (Sarya Al Suwas), Nadran Aalaya (Asi El Hellani).**

As composer & producer, television includes: **Al Hosrom Al Shami.**

Rizan is a composer, musician and producer. He is responsible for hundreds of Syrian recording industry productions as well as compositions and themes for television and cinema. His first solo album, The King of Keyboard, received critical acclaim internationally. Rizan and Mark Gergis have worked together in many capacities since 2006. Mark produced five anthology collections and live recordings of Rizan's musical collaborations with singer Omar Souleyman.

Yasmine Seale
(Associate Translator)

Yasmine is a writer and translator based in Istanbul. She translated an earlier version of Goats for a rehearsed reading at the Royal Court in 2016. Goats is the first complete work she has translated for the stage.

Quang Kien Van
(Movement Director)

As choreographer, for the Royal Court: **Bunny Dance (Beyond the Court).**

As performer, for the Royal Court: **Teh Internet Is Serious Business.**

As choreographer, other theatre includes: **Lunar Shadows (QKV Projects); SHAME: Parts One & Two (Bang Bang Bang Group); Lunar Orbits, Lunar Corps (Chinese Arts Space).**

As performer, dance includes: **Miaan, SisGo, Innocence (Scottish Dance); Blake Diptych, Disgo (Darkin Ensemble); View from the Shore (Jacky Lansley Dance); O (Michael Clark Company); Mystere (Cirque du Soleil); Interview, Flying the Rainbow (Oxytoc Dance Project);Tchaikovsky Trilogy, Hamlet, Midnight Express, Romeo & Juliet, Kermesseni Brugge, The King, HC Anderson (Peter Schaufuss Ballet); Othello, XXX CLOSEUP, Where I End & We Begin, Ultimate Ophelia, Loose Ends, Magma (Skanes Dansteater); Matthew Bourne's Swan Lake (Adventures in Motion Pictures).**

As performer, opera includes: **Skin Deep (Opera North); Ariodante (ENO).**

THE ROYAL COURT THEATRE

The Royal Court Theatre is the writers' theatre. It is a leading force in world theatre for energetically cultivating writers – undiscovered, emerging and established.

Through the writers, the Royal Court is at the forefront of creating restless, alert, provocative theatre about now. We open our doors to the unheard voices and free thinkers that, through their writing, change our way of seeing.

Over 120,000 people visit the Royal Court in Sloane Square, London, each year and many thousands more see our work elsewhere through transfers to the West End and New York, UK and international tours, digital platforms, our residencies across London, and our site-specific work. Through all our work we strive to inspire audiences and influence future writers with radical thinking and provocative discussion.

The Royal Court's extensive development activity encompasses a diverse range of writers and artists and includes an ongoing programme of writers' attachments, readings, workshops and playwriting groups. Twenty years of the International Department's pioneering work around the world means the Royal Court has relationships with writers on every continent.

Within the past sixty years, John Osborne, Samuel Beckett, Arnold Wesker, Ann Jellicoe, Howard Brenton and David Hare have started their careers at the Court. Many others including Caryl Churchill, Athol Fugard, Mark Ravenhill, Simon Stephens, debbie tucker green, Sarah Kane – and, more recently, Lucy Kirkwood, Nick Payne, Penelope Skinner and Alistair McDowall – have followed.

The Royal Court has produced many iconic plays from Laura Wade's **Posh** to Jez Butterworth's **Jerusalem** and Martin McDonagh's **Hangmen**.

Royal Court plays from every decade are now performed on stage and taught in classrooms and universities across the globe.

It is because of this commitment to the writer that we believe there is no more important theatre in the world than the Royal Court.

Supported using public funding by
ARTS COUNCIL ENGLAND

INTERNATIONAL PLAYWRIGHTS
AT THE ROYAL COURT THEATRE

Over the last two decades the Royal Court Theatre has led the way in the development and production of new international plays, facilitating work at grass-roots level and developing exchanges which brings UK writers and directors to work with emerging artists around the world. Through a programme of long-term workshops and residencies, in London and abroad, a creative dialogue now exists with theatre practitioners from over 70 countries, working in over 40 languages, most recently Argentina, Chile, China, Cuba, Georgia, India, Lebanon, Mexico, Palestine, Russia, South Africa, Syria, Turkey, Ukraine, Uruguay and Zimbabwe. All of these development projects are supported by the Genesis Foundation and the British Council.

The Royal Court Theatre has produced dozens of new international plays through this programme since 1997, most recently **Bad Roads** by Natal'ya Vorozhbit (Ukraine) and **B** by Guillermo Calderón (Chile) in 2017, **I See You** by Mongiwekhaya (South Africa) in 2016, **Fireworks** by Dalia Taha (Palestine) in 2015, **The Djinns of Eidgah** by Abhishek Majumdar (India) and **A Time to Reap** by Anna Wakulik (Poland) in 2013, **Remembrance Day** by Aleksey Scherbak (Latvia) and **Our Private Life** by Pedro Miguel Rozo (Colombia) in 2011, and **Disconnect** by Anupama Chandrasekhar (India) in 2010.

ROYAL COURT AND SYRIA

The Royal Court began working with writers in Syria in 2006 with a project in Damascus led by David Greig and Sacha Wares. In 2007 five Syrian writers travelled to London for further development of their plays at the Royal Court. This was followed by the start of a major regional project supported by the British Council which included three Syrian writers among emerging playwrights from seven different countries. The first phase of this project took place in Damascus in April 2007 and was led by April De Angelis, David Greig and Elyse Dodgson. In 2008 **I Come from There: New Plays from the Arab World** was presented in the Jerwood Theatre Upstairs and featured the play **Withdrawal** by Syrian playwright Mohammad Al Attar, translated by Clem Naylor. This was published by Nick Hern Books in 2010. At the end of 2011 Mohammad Al Attar's **Online** was presented as part of a programme of new short plays from the Arab world called **After the Spring** in the Jerwood Theatre Upstairs.

Many Syrian writers/directors have taken part in the Royal Court International Residency since 2005. They include Omar Abu Sada, Abdullah Al Kafri and Wael Qadour. In 2014 a new project began, supported by the British Council, with writers from Lebanon and Syria near Beirut. This was led by David Greig, Sam Holcroft and Elyse Dodgson. Six Syrian writers from inside and outside the country developed new plays over a period of two years. Two plays from Syria were presented as works in progress as part of **Told from the Inside** in the Jerwood Theatre Downstairs in March 2016: **The Final Return** by Ghiath Mhithawi and **Goats** by Liwaa Yazji.

Established by John Studzinski 16 years ago, the Genesis Foundation works in partnership with the leaders of prestigious UK arts organisations such as the Royal Court, The Sixteen, Welsh National Opera and the Young Vic. Its largest funding commitment is to programmes that support directors, playwrights and musicians in the early stages of their professional lives.

In addition it awards scholarships to exceptional student actors at LAMDA and commissions stimulating new works, from choral compositions to light installations.

In 2015 the Genesis Foundation launched its first partnership outside the UK, funding residencies for playwrights at New York's Signature Theatre.

Genesis
FOUNDATION

ROYA

COMING UP AT THE ROYAL COURT

6 Dec–23 Dec
Grimly Handsome
By Julia Jarcho

8 Jan–20 Jan
My Mum's A Twat
By Anoushka Warden

9 Jan–27 Jan
ROYAL COURT THEATRE, OUT OF JOINT AND
OCTAGON THEATRE BOLTON
Rita, Sue and Bob Too
By Andrea Dunbar

31 Jan–10 Mar
Gundog
By Simon Longman

8 Feb–10 Mar
Girls & Boys
By Dennis Kelly

21 Mar–7 Apr
ECLIPSE THEATRE COMPANY AND
ROYAL EXCHANGE THEATRE
Black Men Walking
By Testament

Tickets from £12
royalcourttheatre.com

Supported using public funding by
ARTS COUNCIL ENGLAND

Sloane Square London, SW1W 8AS   Sloane Square
Victoria Station   royalcourt   royalcourttheatre

GUNDOG is part of the Royal Court's Jerwood
New Playwrights programme, supported by

JERWOOD **CHARITABLE** FOUNDATION

ROYAL COURT SUPPORTERS

The Royal Court is a registered charity and not-for-profit company. We need to raise £1.5 million every year in addition to our core grant from the Arts Council and our ticket income to achieve what we do.

We have significant and longstanding relationships with many generous organisations and individuals who provide vital support. Royal Court supporters enable us to remain the writers' theatre, find stories from everywhere and create theatre for everyone.

We can't do it without you.

PUBLIC FUNDING

Arts Council England, London
British Council

TRUSTS & FOUNDATIONS

The Bryan Adams Charitable Trust
The Austin & Hope Pilkington Trust
Martin Bowley Charitable Trust
Gerald Chapman Fund
CHK Charities
The City Bridge Trust
The Clifford Chance Foundation
Cockayne - Grants for the Arts
The Nöel Coward Foundation
Cowley Charitable Trust
The Eranda Rothschild Foundation
Lady Antonia Fraser for The Pinter Commission
Genesis Foundation
The Golden Bottle Trust
The Haberdashers' Company
The Paul Hamlyn Foundation
Roderick & Elizabeth Jack
Jerwood Charitable Foundation
Kirsh Foundation
The Mackintosh Foundation
The Andrew Lloyd Webber Foundation
The London Community Foundation
John Lyon's Charity
Clare McIntyre's Bursary

The Andrew W. Mellon Foundation
The David & Elaine Potter Foundation
The Richard Radcliffe Charitable Trust
Rose Foundation
Royal Victoria Hall Foundation
The Sackler Trust
The Sobell Foundation
John Thaw Foundation
The Wellcome Trust
The Garfield Weston Foundation

CORPORATE SPONSORS

Aqua Financial Solutions Ltd
Bloomberg
Cadogan Estates
Colbert
Edwardian Hotels, London
Fever-Tree
Gedye & Sons
Kirkland & Ellis International LLP
Kudos
MAC
Room One
Sister Pictures
Sky Drama

BUSINESS MEMBERS

Annoushka
Auerbach & Steele Opticians
CNC – Communications & Network Consulting
Cream
Lansons
Left Bank Pictures
Rockspring Property Investment Managers
Tetragon Financial Group

For more information or to become a foundation or business supporter contact Camilla Start: camillastart@ royalcourttheatre. com/020 7565 5064.

INDIVIDUAL SUPPORTERS

Artistic Director's Circle
Eric Abraham
Carolyn Bennett
Samantha & Richard
  Campbell-Breeden
Cas Donald
Lydia & Manfred Gorvy
Charles Holloway
Luke Johnson
Jack & Linda Keenan
Angelie & Shafin Moledina
Miles Morland
Anatol Orient
NoraLee & Jon Sedmak
Deborah Shaw
  & Stephen Marquardt
Jan & Michael Topham
Matthew & Sian Westerman
Mahdi Yahya

Writers' Circle
Scott M. Delman
Jane Featherstone
Jean & David Grier
Mandeep Manku
Emma O'Donoghue
Mr & Mrs Sandy Orr
Carol Sellars
Maria Sukkar
Maureen & Tony Wheeler
The Wilhelm Helmut Trust
Anonymous

Directors' Circle
William & Asli Arah
Dr Kate Best
Katie Bradford
Piers Butler
Chris & Alison Cabot
Emma & Phil Coffer
Joachim Fleury
Piers & Melanie Gibson
Louis Greig
David & Claudia Harding
Roderick & Elizabeth Jack
Melanie J Johnson
Nicola Kerr
Mrs Joan Kingsley
Emma Marsh
Rachel Mason
Andrew & Ariana Rodger
Anonymous

Platinum Members
Moira Andreae
Nick Archdale
Elizabeth & Adam Bandeen
Clive & Helena Butler

Gavin & Lesley Casey
Sarah & Philippe Chappatte
Michael & Arlene Cohrs
Clyde Cooper
Mrs Lara Cross
T Cross
Andrew & Amanda Cryer
Shane & Catherine Cullinane
Alison Davies
Matthew Dean
Sarah Denning
Cherry & Rob Dickins
Denise & Randolph Dumas
Robyn Durie
Mark & Sarah Evans
Sally & Giles Everist
Celeste & Peter Fenichel
Emily Fletcher
The Edwin Fox Foundation
Dominic & Claire Freemantle
Beverley Gee
Nick & Julie Gould
The Richard Grand Foundation
Jill Hackel & Andrzej Zarzycki
Carol Hall
Peter & Debbie Hargreaves
Sam & Caroline Haubold
Mr & Mrs Gordon Holmes
Dr Timothy Hyde
Damien Hyland
Trevor Ingman
Amanda & Chris Jennings
Ralph Kanter
David P Kaskel
  & Christopher A Teano
Vincent & Amanda Keaveny
Peter & Maria Kellner
Mr & Mrs Pawel Kisielewski
Rosemary Leith
Kathryn Ludlow
The Maplescombe Trust
Christopher Marek
  Rencki
Mrs Janet Martin
Andrew McIver
David & Elizabeth Miles
David Mills
Barbara Minto
M.E. Murphy Altschuler
Siobhan Murphy
Peter & Maggie Murray-Smith
Georgia Oetker
Adam Oliver-Watkins
Crispin Osborne
Andrea & Hilary Ponti
Theo Priovolos
Greg & Karen Reid
Paul & Gill Robinson
Corinne Rooney
Sir Paul & Lady Ruddock
William & Hilary Russell

Sally & Anthony Salz
Jane Scobie
Anita Scott
Bhags Sharma
Dr. Wendy Sigle
Andy Simpkin
Brian Smith
John Soler & Meg Morrison
Kim Taylor-Smith
Mrs Caroline Thomas
Alex Timken
The Ulrich Family
Monica B Voldstad
Arrelle & François Von Hurter
Anne-Marie Williams
Sir Robert & Lady Wilson
Anonymous

With thanks to our Friends, Silver and Gold Members whose support we greatly appreciate.

DEVELOPMENT COUNCIL

Majella Altschuler
Piers Butler
Chris Cabot
Cas Donald
Celeste Fenichel
Tim Hincks
Emma Marsh
Angelie Moledina
Anatol Orient
Andrew Rodger
Sian Westerman

Our Supporters contribute to all aspects of the Royal Court's work including: productions, commissions, writers groups, International, Young Court and Beyond the Court programmes, creative posts, the Trainee scheme and access initiatives as well as providing in-kind support.

For more information or to become a Supporter please contact Charlotte Cole: charlottecole@royalcourttheatre.com/020 7565 5049.

Supported using public funding by
ARTS COUNCIL ENGLAND

"There are no spaces, no rooms in my opinion, with a greater legacy of fearlessness, truth and clarity than this space."

Simon Stephens, Associate Playwright

The Royal Court invests in the future of the theatre, offering writers the support, time and resources to find their voices and tell their stories, asking the big questions and responding to the issues of the moment.

As a registered charity, the Royal Court relies on the generous support of individuals to seek out, develop and nurture new voices. Please join us in Writing The Future by donating today.

You can donate online at royalcourttheatre.com/donate or via our donation box in the Bar & Kitchen.

We can't do it without you.

Writing the Future

To find out more about the different ways in which you can be involved please contact Charlotte Cole on 020 7565 5049 / charlottecole@royalcourttheatre.com

The English Stage Company at the Royal Court Theatre is a registered charity (No. 231242).

GOATS

Liwaa Yazji

Translated by Katharine Halls

Acknowledgements

With thanks to the Royal Court and to my fellow participants in the Royal Court/British Council New Writing for Theatre Project (Syria & Lebanon).

Special thanks to Mohammed Abu Laban.

L.Y.

4

Characters

ABU FIRAS, *late sixties*
IMM GHASSAN, *early seventies, mother of Ghassan
    and Adnan*
ADNAN, *early thirties, Imm Ghassan's son*
ZAHRA, *mid-twenties, pregnant, Adnan's wife*
ABU AL-TAYYIB, *late forties, chair of the local branch
    of the Party*
IMM AL-TAYYIB, *mid-forties, Abu al-Tayyib's wife, long
    dark hair*
MUDAR, *teenage, Abu al-Tayyib's son*
TEENAGERS: FADI, JUDE *and* SAMI
IMM NABIL, *late sixties, blind*
ABU KARIM, *morgue attendant*
STATE TV CREW: PRESENTER, CAMERAMAN *and*
    TECHNICIANS
VILLAGERS: ABU LU'AY, IMM MAZEN, IMM AZIZ,
    ABU ALA' *and* IMM ALA', ABU JAMAL *and* IMM
    JAMAL, IMM MARWAN, SHEIKH ABU SALAM, ABU
    AHMAD, ABU MUHAMMAD 1, ABU MUHAMMAD 2,
    ABU AL-REEM, ABU SAMER *and* IMM SAMER, ABU
    SALMA *and* IMM SALMA, ABU RAMI *and* IMM RAMI
    and IMM NADER
STATE OFFICIALS: MEN FROM THE MUNICIPALITY,
    MEMBERS OF THE PARTY BRANCH, SECRETARIES
    OF STATE, HEADTEACHERS, COMMITTEE CHAIRS,
    REPORT WRITERS, BODYGUARDS
OLDER MEN
WOMEN *of all ages*
CHILDREN

And GOATS

Note on Play

A village in Syria, 2016.

The audience may be treated as villagers.

Act One may begin as the audience are entering the theatre, as if they are participating in the ceremony. The same goes for the final act.

The Party Office and Abu al-Tayyib's house are in the same building.

Acts Fifteen and Sixteen take place simultaneously.

The sounds of fighting, missiles and explosions gradually become clearer and clearer over the course of the play.

From the time the goats appear, their bleating is constant in every scene.

The footage that appears on the screen is a combination of live recording from the stage, videos prepared in advance, and archival material.

'On stage and screen' indicates that the footage showing on screen is being recorded live from the action on stage. The camera affects the gathered villagers' behaviour. When they are within the camera's range, they become noticeably better behaved and less sloppy.

The teenagers are not addressed by name.

'Imm' means 'mother (of)', and 'Abu' means 'father (of)'.

The English translation is shorter than the original play in Arabic.

This text went to press before the end of rehearsals and so may differ slightly from the play as performed.

Scene One – Funeral

*The main square. Afternoon. The screen is initially off.
Funereal music. Coffins slowly appear, carried by* MEN *and*
TEENAGERS, *who converge and place the coffins on the
ground. There is scarcely enough space for all the coffins,
which continue to appear.*

*The first coffins are fully draped in clean flags with bright
colours, and some with bouquets and wreaths. As more coffins
appear, the flags grow more faded and tattered, and smaller, so
that the coffins aren't properly covered. Likewise, the flowers are
less and less frequent; some of the final coffins have been strewn
with wildflowers. One of the coffins appears to have common
mallow laid on it.* ABU FIRAS *accompanies the coffin of his son,
Firas, never leaving its side, as he stands waiting impatiently.*

*People wait respectfully, but as time passes they start to shift
restlessly. The sound of ululating fills the space as the* WOMEN
*enter, weeping and wearing black, in a funeral tradition that is
reminiscent of a wedding. The* WOMEN *try to squeeze their way
in to the limited space. The* MUNICIPALITY MEN, *the* PARTY
MEMBERS *and their* BODYGUARDS *arrive.* JUDE *and* SAMI
*enter, carrying a large tray that bears an enormous, homemade-
looking cake in the shape of a pair of military boots, and another
in the shape of a bullet.* VILLAGERS *try to make space for them
to set down the tray in its place, all eyes watching them intently.*
JUDE *and* SAMI *are followed by a little* BOY *and* GIRL *dressed
as bride and groom, shyly accompanying the tray. They wear hats
with model military boots on them.*

*The screen suddenly turns on, showing the preparations
underway in the mobile production truck. It looks as if the
camera has turned on without the* CAMERAMAN *noticing.
It moves about erratically, showing the crowds and then the*
PRESENTER *doing her hair.*

PRESENTER. Can we get started?

ABU AL-TAYYIB *begins his speech suddenly and without preamble.*

ABU AL-TAYYIB (*on stage and screen. With a melodious voice and polished delivery*). In the name of our innocent martyrs, the pride of our nation. We gather today to remember our nation's martyrs, the brave members of the army and security services... And, of course, the others... For the sake of this precious nation, we stand for a minute's silence.

Silence. On screen, close-up shots of the crowd give the impression of a reverent, awestruck atmosphere.

On the third of this month, armed terrorists assassinated our chief nuclear adviser. He died at home, here in our village. Two days before, armed terrorists assassinated a Professor of Chemistry. She was Dean of her faculty and had won the State Prize. These atrocities happened in a single week. The terrorists are targeting our best people – they hate knowledge, and they fear our freedom.

We are fighting back, and we have inflicted severe losses on the terrorists. But, in the last week alone, we have lost over eight hundred men defending our front line. Soldiers and civilians. That's in one week, in a war that's already lasted seven years.

We grieve for them. Our grief will not be diminished by hatred or revenge. But we are fighting on behalf of the entire civilised world. We shall kill and we shall be killed, but the nation will never die.

ABU KARIM (*loudly*). It's a conspiracy! Against all of us.

ABU AL-TAYYIB (*continuing*). And your children are our children. Who among us has not lost a son? Who has not lost a brother or a husband? Yet now, here they are, returning to us. Here is our gentle Aziz. He fought to the very last. Aziz destroyed an entire terrorist cell. And now he is a great martyr.

IMM AZIZ *ululates tearfully.*

ABU LU'AY (*gesturing to the cake*). I swear on this blessing. My son Lu'ay, he called me from the front line. He said, 'Dad, I wish you were here. To see what I'm doing to these cowards.' And now, he is a martyr. My son, all our sons, they are willing to give their lives for this nation. If we won't pay with our blood, who will?

ABU AL-TAYYIB (*to ABU LU'AY*). Absolutely! Your son has brought glory on your household, Abu Lu'ay, congratulations. (*To* IMM MARWAN.) Imm Marwan, your son was worth his weight in gold. What an honour for his young bride! (*To* IMM GHASSAN.) Imm Ghassan, your son was an officer, a pilot who never feared death, who wiped out terrorists from the air. You must be so proud that his home is now in the heavens.

ZAHRA *ululates*. IMM GHASSAN *shows little reaction.*

ZAHRA. My mother-in-law, Imm Ghassan, has sworn never to speak again. Never to speak another word, until she has avenged her son. We will never forgive the enemy for his death!

The VILLAGERS *look surprised at this news. They whisper among themselves.* IMM GHASSAN *avoids their looks and questions.*

ABU FIRAS *is about to speak, but he is cut off immediately by* ABU AL-TAYYIB.

ABU AL-TAYYIB. Abu Firas, you must be so proud of your courageous son. People in neighbouring villages were shielding terrorists and Firas tore those terrorists limb from limb. They are now so afraid of Firas, they dread hearing his name.

ABU FIRAS *attempts to speak.*

Now, I won't keep you for much longer. You are all waiting impatiently to see your beloved sons embrace the soil of the land they held so dear. Allow me a few final words before we make our way to the cemetery. My good people. My dear, suffering people –

ABU FIRAS (*interrupting quietly but clearly*). Enough!

VILLAGERS (*not in unison*). Yeah… Enough! No more terrorism! Down with traitors! Enough!

ABU FIRAS (*correcting himself*). Enough of this madness!

    ABU AL-TAYYIB *is taken aback. Shock and consternation ripple through the crowd.*

    On screen, the camera cuts to show the faces of the TEENAGERS. *They immediately stand up straighter.*

ABU AL-TAYYIB. What do you mean, Abu Firas? I don't follow!

ABU FIRAS (*shaken but unhesitating*). Think about it, and you will see what I mean.

    On screen, IMM GHASSAN*'s impassive face. She watches her son Ghassan's coffin unflinchingly. One of the* BODYGUARDS *places himself in front of* ABU FIRAS *so as to block him from sight, but* ABU AL-TAYYIB *gestures to him to move aside.*

VOICE (*from the production truck*). Shall we take this off the air?

    The screen displays close-ups of the coffins, and photographs of the martyrs held up by VILLAGERS *in the crowd, accompanied by mournful music.*

    On stage, the VILLAGERS *are restive and uneasy.*

ABU FIRAS. Abu al-Tayyib, I am not here to celebrate. You know that very well. My son is dead. A month ago, he left out of the blue. You all know I've been looking for him. Someone took him away from me, and now he's been brought back in a sealed box! Where is Firas?

IMM RAMI. A sealed box!

OFFICIAL (*to a* BODYGUARD). Get them to stop the cameras. We don't want a fuss.

ABU AL-TAYYIB (*aside*). No, we can't do that. People will be expecting the evening programme. (*To the* PRESENTER.) Get on with it! (*To* ABU FIRAS.) Abu Firas, I know you

well. I am sure you're saying all this out of grief over Firas.
We understand this is a cruel moment. It blinds you, makes
you completely lose your bearings. Abu Firas, come back to
your senses.

ABU FIRAS. These are our children. Not a TV programme.

Some VILLAGERS *elbow towards* ABU FIRAS *and attempt
to calm him with pleasantries. The screen shows snow, as if
there has been a technical glitch, then cuts abruptly to footage
of military parades and nationalist propaganda videos.*

Why don't you ask *him* about this?

ABU SALMA. He hasn't been right since his son joined the
army.

ABU FIRAS. My son didn't join the army. My son was stolen.

ABU AHMAD. Now you sound like one of those human-rights
people.

PRESENTER. I'm completely lost.

MUDAR *starts to explain.*

ABU AL-TAYYIB (*to* MUDAR). You keep quiet. (*To* ABU
FIRAS.) Where has this come from?

ABU FIRAS. Put yourselves in my shoes.

ABU RAMI. But we're all in the same boat.

IMM MARWAN. One thing I know, for sure, is that my son is
no more important or precious than the nation. Anyone who
says otherwise is a traitor and a hypocrite.

IMM JAMAL. Poison!

The screen shows shots of IMM MARWAN *looking sad,
with accompanying music. It pans across the* VILLAGERS'
*faces. It then cuts to show the cake, which is no longer on
stage.*

ABU SAMER. Abu Firas's father was a coffin-bearer for our
late president. How can his son turn out to be so nasty and
ungrateful?

ABU SALMA. War is natural. We didn't invent it! It's nature.
Nature's way to defend itself against human stupidity.
Human beings pop out more and more babies, so the ground
swallows them up. I mean, some day we're all going to die.

IMM SALMA (*aside, to* ABU SALMA). Dearest, please shut
up!

ABU FIRAS. Why don't you defend your children, like you
defend your country?

IMM ALA'. Abu Firas, listen! Firas died with my son. They
were together. Ala' called me, that very day. He told me to
pray for him. He said, 'Mum, pray for me, and for the boys!'
(*Waves a photo*.) See how handsome he was! How smart his
suit was!

ABU ALA' (*reproachfully*). Stop replying to him!

ABU FIRAS. No, they came to your doorstep, and they handed
over your son's things. You ululated. Then they parade you
about with the 'happy news'! Literally, that's all you know
about how your son died.

BODYGUARDS *move roughly to stop* ABU FIRAS *from
finishing*. ABU AL-TAYYIB *gestures to them to take it easy.*

(*To* ABU AL-TAYYIB.) You can't get rid of me that easily,
Abu al-Tayyib. Now listen, and listen carefully. Firas is not
in that coffin. Until I see his body, I can't begin to accept
that is my son. (*To the others*.) These are not your children.
The coffins are empty. We don't know who – or what – is
inside them.

ABU AL-TAYYIB. Wow. You're heading for the mental
hospital. And you're usually so reasonable.

BODYGUARD. Sir, we really need to do something.

ABU AL-TAYYIB. We certainly do. We can't have people
thinking we're scared of him.

ABU FIRAS (*to* ABU AL-TAYYIB). Abu al-Tayyib, you
promised me I could see my son. If you had kept your
promise, you wouldn't need to –

ABU AL-TAYYIB. I have never made any promises to you.
(*To all the* VILLAGERS.) Tell me, who believes these
ridiculous lies? (*Silence*.) Anyone else want to embarrass us
all, on live television?

ABU FIRAS. I want to see my son. I've been trying since
I found out he'd been killed. But you're avoiding me.

ABU MUHAMMAD 1. Why should they let *you* see your son,
you and no one else? Why are *you* so special?

ABU AHMAD (*quietly*). Because Abu Firas is the son of a big
shot. He can't take it.

IMM NADER. Martyrdom makes all people equal!

ABU AL-REEM. If they open one single coffin, I will empty
my gun into his head.

ABU AL-TAYYIB (*addressing the families*). Why do any of
our children give up their lives?

ALL (*in unison*). For the nation.

ABU AL-TAYYIB. These are the laws of nature and history.
Who are you to change them?

ABU FIRAS. Abu al-Tayyib, for the last time. You can put an
end to this.

ABU AL-TAYYIB (*to* ABU FIRAS). No. You are making a big
mistake, accusing us of being traitors.

ABU AL-TAYYIB *gives a signal to the* BODYGUARDS,
who move closer to ABU FIRAS, *ready to hustle him away.*

ABU FIRAS. Nothing will move me. Imm Ghassan, this is not
the time to keep quiet. Abu Lu'ay, Imm Aziz! Why are you
standing for this?

ZAHRA. You are making a mockery of your son's sacrifice.

ABU FIRAS. Imm Ghassan, say something.

ABU AL-TAYYIB. Abu Firas, the only person you are thinking
about is yourself. Every mother has a happy memory of their

son. (*To the* VILLAGERS.) Who wants to see their son now, and to desecrate the sanctity of the coffin? Show yourselves!

No response.

ABU FIRAS. Cowards!

ABU AL-TAYYIB. Abu Firas, you've lost. Now, get out of here. A martyr belongs to his nation. Not to you.

ABU FIRAS (*makes his way towards Firas's coffin*). Over my dead body.

ABU AL-TAYYIB. Be careful what you wish for.

ABU FIRAS. I cannot consent to this. Sheikh, this is supposed to be your job. Religion says no one can bury my son without my consent... Tell them!

SHEIKH (*hesitantly*). Abu Firas, I implore you –

ABU FIRAS. Answer me out loud. I want everyone to hear. I asked you before, and you said I was right. No one can bury someone's child without their permission. It goes against the shari'a. And who decides the shari'a?

SHEIKH (*even more hesitantly*). Well, the shari'a cannot be questioned –

ABU AL-TAYYIB. So, you two plotted this in advance, did you?

SHEIKH. Comrade Abu al-Tayyib, God forbid! Abu Firas asked me, and I told hi–

ABU FIRAS. Hear that, everyone? If you want to see your son, then ask the Sheikh.

Pause.

ABU AL-TAYYIB *surveys the crowd for any response.*
The VILLAGERS *are frightened and hesitant. Silence.*
ABU AL-TAYYIB *smiles, mocking* ABU FIRAS.

Shame!

ABU AL-TAYYIB. Abu Firas, your little performance is over. (*To the* PRESENTER.) Now, let's get started.

ABU AL-TAYYIB *turns away, gesturing to everyone to resume the ceremony.* ABU FIRAS *remains uncomprehending.* ABU AL-TAYYIB *gestures to the* BODYGUARDS *to surround* ABU FIRAS *and discreetly prevent him from talking any further.*

(*Resuming his speech.*) I do apologise. This is a difficult time for all of us. It has a strange effect on some people, and we need to be tolerant.

The screen shows ABU AL-TAYYIB*'s face again. He returns to the formal language of the script for his speech.*

After this emotional interlude, let me remind you that today's gathering is a special one. It is a fitting opportunity to announce we have agreed to your demands – to lower the minimum age for volunteers from eighteen to sixteen. Long live you the people! Long live the nation! And long live its leader! Please, you are most welcome to register your son's name and age.

ABU AL-TAYYIB *leaves the podium immediately, looking uncomfortable. He beckons to* ABU MUHAMMAD 1, *who starts to register the volunteers.*

On screen, close-ups of people queueing to sign up, eagerly but in an orderly fashion.

On stage, some VILLAGERS *are hesitant, almost imperceptibly.* ABU AL-TAYYIB *leaves, gesturing to* MUDAR *to get to work.* MUDAR *goes to the coffins, and starts collecting up the wreaths and flags ready to be packed away.*

MEN *carry away the coffins.* ABU FIRAS *watches as one coffin after another disappears.* ABU AL-TAYYIB *leaves with the* OFFICIALS.

ABU SALMA. For goodness' sake, let the poor man see his son.

ABU AL-REEM. So every crazy person gets what they want?

ABU MUHAMMAD 1. I've got too many names here. Has someone put down their son's name twice?

ABU JAMAL. Maybe Abu Firas has got a point.

ABU LU'AY. That bastard has got you brainwashed.

IMM JAMAL *throws herself on a coffin so that the* MEN *can't remove it.*

IMM JAMAL. If they are going to open Firas's coffin, they have to open them all.

IMM GHASSAN *moves away, leaning on* ZAHRA *for support. As* IMM GHASSAN *leaves,* ABU FIRAS *looks on despondently.*

On screen, PRESENTER *smoothly and professionally covers up the disorder.*

PRESENTER (*on screen*). We have been reporting live from the ceremony to mark the sacrifices made by the nation's martyrs. Today's wedding was held to honour these men. They were plucked in the flower of their youth – Aziz, Jamal, Ala', Lu'ay, Mazen, Marwan, Ghassan. Many names, but their sacrifice is small price – for the good of the nation.

Today, Firas, a dutiful son of the land, celebrated his sixteenth birthday, embraced by the soil of his dear country. His message, written in his blood, is short but sweet. 'With our souls, with our lives – we sacrifice ourselves for you, O nation.'

On screen, close-up of a photo of young Firas, surrounded by flowers. The 'Martyr's Anthem' plays. The cake is in front of the photo. ABU FIRAS *sees the photo on screen, and gets angrier.*

ABU FIRAS. Where the hell did you get that photo? Firas!

The PRESENTER *appears on screen again.* ABU FIRAS *can still be seen and heard yelling behind her.* WOMEN *start to ululate to cover up the sound.*

PRESENTER. We can see the joy and pride of the families at the sacrifice of their menfolk. It is mingled with grief – for the loss of a father, a husband, a son.

Here is the father of one martyr. Abu Firas prefers to be silent today, respecting the sanctity of mourning. Here is Abu Firas, embracing a photograph of his beloved son. Happy birthday to your son, dear Firas!

ABU FIRAS. Lies! It is not his birthday. Where have you taken him?

ABU FIRAS *scrambles towards the* PRESENTER, *but* BODYGUARDS *hold him back.*

On screen, archival footage shows mothers bidding farewell to martyred sons.

On stage, PRESENTER *reads from a piece of paper. It is a poem, 'The Loveliest of Mothers' by Hasan 'Abd Allah.*

PRESENTER. The loveliest of mothers is the mother who awaits her son / He returns a martyr. / She sheds two tears and a rose / And she does not hide herself in mourning.

ABU RAMI. Where has the cake got to?

On stage, almost everyone has left.

JUDE *and* SAMI *hurry to help carry Firas's coffin. They react to its heavy weight.* ABU FIRAS *grasps at the coffin and holds on to it tenaciously.*

JUDE *and* SAMI *leave.* ABU FIRAS *follows the coffin.*

MUDAR *and* FADI *are left alone.* FADI *watches silently.*

MUDAR. We should've helped them, it was heavy. (*Pause.*) You scared?

FADI. We'll be next. Now that we're allowed to fight.

MUDAR. What you up to later?

FADI. Same as usual.

MUDAR. Same as usual.

MUDAR *takes a television remote control from his pocket and, indifferently, switches off the screen. Everything stops. Darkness.*

Light and white noise from the screen. Silence.

Scene Two – Alone

IMM GHASSAN*'s house. Evening. A single light bulb on.*
IMM GHASSAN *sits outside the front door, counting her prayer
beads. Her daughter-in-law* ZAHRA *knots black shoelaces
together into a long yarn. The sound of a radio can be heard
getting closer.* ZAHRA *leaps up, clutching her things. She waits
for* IMM GHASSAN *to go inside, but* IMM GHASSAN *pays her
no attention and remains where she is.* ZAHRA *is annoyed at
her, and defiantly goes inside alone.*

From the nearby hill comes the light of a torch. ABU FIRAS
approaches on foot. He shines the torch towards IMM
GHASSAN, *who glances at him, then returns to her reverie.
He comes up to her. He pulls up a wicker chair and sits down.
He turns off the torch. Silence.* ABU FIRAS *takes out a pack of
tobacco and rolls a cigarette.*

ABU FIRAS. I can't stay in the house by myself. I can't go into
his room. Even his friends are staying away. Abu al-Tayyib's
men came over today. Can you believe it? They knocked at
the door, they asked me to donate Firas's things. Did they
take Ghassan's things?

IMM GHASSAN *doesn't reply. Pause.*

I did what any parent would do. Why did you let them bury
Ghassan without seeing him? Why didn't you take a stand?
Look me in the eye, tell me you didn't want to see him. You
still refuse to speak? Or you just don't want to talk to me?

The power goes out. IMM GHASSAN *bangs on the ground
with her stick.*

Do you think your silence will change anything?

ZAHRA *emerges from the house, carrying a candle. She
places it on the floor between them.*

ZAHRA (*in an unfriendly tone*). Nice to see you. My
condolences.

ABU FIRAS. No sugar, thanks.

ZAHRA *goes back inside, annoyed.*

(*Softly.*) If it's just me, they'll call me crazy. But everyone respects you. Abu al-Tayyib can't say 'no' to you. Do you believe me when I say he promised me? (*Pause.*) Imm Ghassan, you are the only one who remembers what it was like before, after those crooks took power. Why are you waiting?

ZAHRA (*from inside*). She won't speak until Adnan has got revenge for his brother.

ABU FIRAS (*to* IMM GHASSAN). Is it true what she says, your daughter-in-law? Tell me. I won't say anything. No one will know. (*Pause.*) I've just been to the hospital. They've got him there, but they won't let me in. I've been going every day, since they told me he was dead. Maybe they'll bring him in, and I'll see him. But there are so many bodies. (*Pause.*) We know nothing. We are pathetic. (*Pause.*) Do you know how Ghassan was killed? The details? Your son was an officer, not some clueless first-timer. (*Pause.*) We never imagined our sons could kill, or be killed. (*Angry, raising his voice.*) Say something! I can't do this on my own.

ZAHRA *enters crossly with the tea.*

ZAHRA (*beat*). You know, talking about the dead is like eating their flesh.

IMM GHASSAN *gives her a warning look.* ABU FIRAS *angrily picks up his cup of tea.*

(*To* IMM GHASSAN.) What? So here he is, teaching us to speak out about injustice. A young soldier is dead. And his father talks like this. He lacks respect for his own martyr, but he can show some respect for ours.

ZAHRA *goes inside.*

ABU FIRAS (*directed at* ZAHRA). What if it were your son?

Pause. ABU FIRAS *and* IMM GHASSAN *are alone together again. Silence.*

Before he left, Firas and I had a huge fight. Then he vanished, without a word. I've been out of my mind ever since. We all know they're grabbing young men off buses and taking them to join the army. He might have been forced to join. You know what? He might have been murdered, or kidnapped, and now they're trying to cover it up. Who knows? So many maybes. (*Pause.*) He never said a word about going to fight. He couldn't even make his own dinner. How is he supposed to know how to fight? (*Pause.*) The last time he called me, he sounded so scared. He's a boy, for God's sake! A boy! I'll never forgive them, they brainwashed him. He was saying, 'Dad, I caught some terrorists.' I asked him where, when, who… (*Pause.*) I told him, 'Son, leave them for the dogs. Just come home! Go back to school!' (*Pause.*) You know, he used to sit at the computer. He would say, 'Dad! I'm helping, in the electronic army!' And then he ends up in the real army? What? No, those bastards forced him to sign up.

ZAHRA (*from inside*). All the parents get the call when their boys catch a terrorist. It's a great thing.

ABU FIRAS. You only hear what you want to hear. Firas was scared.

ZAHRA (*from inside*). You must have imagined it. Scared. Maybe he was scared because of you. Other families, they're thrilled to get the news.

ABU FIRAS. What are you talking about? It's a war, not some kind of call-centre!

ZAHRA (*from inside*). The boys are just boasting. It's a phase.

ABU FIRAS. A phase! (*To* ZAHRA *inside.*) Who else rang their family?

ZAHRA (*from inside*). All the martyrs. All the boys who died.

ABU FIRAS. A boy would only call if he was lost and abandoned. (*Pause.*) Did Ghassan ring you?

A gunshot, loud and close. It is followed by screams and wailing. ZAHRA *comes out and runs away in the direction of the sound.*

Finally, ABU FIRAS *and* IMM GHASSAN *are alone.*

Now it's safe to talk. (*Waits. Silence.*) Oh, our children are dying, and you think it's fine, because it's just a phase. You are not saying anything, you must agree. So, help me.

Ululations come from the direction of the gunshot. They stop, and the wailing continues.

You know what that sound means? It means that our children are cheap. (*Pause. Hesitates before continuing.*) I've been on the internet, on Firas's computer, reading the blocked sites. It's not hard to find out what is happening. If we want. If we dare.

ABU FIRAS *takes out a piece of paper from his pocket. It's covered with his handwriting, and folded up small. He unfolds it and offers it to* IMM GHASSAN. *She looks but doesn't reach out to take it. He opens the piece of paper and reads out loud.*

(*Reading.*) 'The regime is responsible for the deaths of thousands. But these thousands are not just statistics. It is cruelty on an industrial scale. They are children. Many parents receive bodies marked by violent torture. Other parents are handed their child's ID card, but they have never seen their body. Some parents were sent only a pile of severed limbs. (*Pause.*) This regime is trivialising murder. Killing for the sake of killing. Leaving fathers without sons.'[1] (*To* IMM GHASSAN.) You see. This is what we are doing, and this is what's happening to us.

ABU FIRAS, *angry and agitated, takes many more folded pieces of paper out of his pocket. He scatters them on the floor where they pile up. Gesturing to the piles of clippings.*

These are the people our children are killing. And the people who are killing our children. Who is the enemy? (*Pause.*) I've seen them on the news. Monsters. Just like us. I expected everyone else to leave me in the lurch today. But not you. You can't fight a battle by not turning up. Isn't that what our children are teaching us?

IMM GHASSAN *doesn't move. Sound of wailing in the distance fades. Pause.* ABU FIRAS *picks up the clippings of paper.*

---

1. Jamal Subh, 'Of fathers without sons: Revolution in the psychology of loss', aljumhuriya.net.

Maybe I should shut up. All those years ago, I missed my chance. I failed to speak when I should have.

IMM GHASSAN *starts to cry silently.*

That's one way of talking.

ABU FIRAS *moves his hand towards his pocket.* IMM GHASSAN *starts up threateningly.*

No more paper, I promise. Just looking for a tissue.

IMM GHASSAN *smiles,* ABU FIRAS *smiles.*

Enter ZAHRA.

IMM GHASSAN *looks at* ZAHRA *questioningly.* ZAHRA *is uncomfortable, not wanting to speak while* ABU FIRAS *is present.*

ZAHRA. It's Yazan. Imm Nabil's grandson. They say he shot himself. While he was cleaning his gun.

ABU FIRAS. Is he badly hurt?

ZAHRA. He's dead.

ABU FIRAS. We never learn. (*To* IMM GHASSAN, *as he gets up to leave.*) Imm Ghassan, don't let me down. I hope Adnan returns safe and sound.

ZAHRA. Let's hope he comes back with his head high.

ABU FIRAS. Let's hope he comes back with his head.

ZAHRA. If I have his child, he will never die.

ABU FIRAS *smiles and sets off.*

IMM GHASSAN *looks at* ZAHRA.

What? He won't starve just because I didn't ask him to stay for dinner. (*Tidies up the tea cup, and sits down in* ABU FIRAS*'s place.*) In a few days, more martyrs will arrive at the National Hospital. Yazan will be taken there. (*Pause.*) There is another reception for the bodies. It will be on TV. (*Pause.*) His granddad wanted him to join the militia. They say the pay is good. (*Pause.*) Poor thing. He must have been

practising with his rifle, and it went off in his face. And now
he's a martyr. Just like his father.

ZAHRA *goes inside.*

(*From inside.*) Can you imagine? That family doesn't have
a single framed photo of Yazan. You have to think about
these things in advance.

IMM GHASSAN *begins to moan softly, in unison with
distant voices. She stops immediately when* ZAHRA *returns
with the clean laundry and starts to hang it out. The laundry
is all men's clothing.* IMM GHASSAN *stares transfixed at
the clothes.*

It's not forecast to rain. Where are Ghassan's other clothes?
I can't find them.

ZAHRA *stops suddenly, as if she's remembered something,
and quickly goes inside. She comes out carrying a large dish
of ice.*

The morgues are full. They'll have to keep Yazan at home.
We're all bringing ice.

Exit ZAHRA. *Pause.*

IMM GHASSAN *goes over to the washing line, smells the
clothing and buries her face in it. Her anger and sadness
become more intense. She picks up a stick, and starts beating
the ground with it. Then she beats herself, moaning silently.
The candle goes out.*

IMM GHASSAN *stops, exhausted, and sits back down.
Pause.*

ZAHRA *returns. She relights the candle. She notices
something odd has happened to* IMM GHASSAN, *who is
dusty, and so is the washing.* ZAHRA *goes into the house.*

(*From inside.*) Oh, there's no end to it. (*Pause.*) I'll have to
wash them all over again. You do that to stop us donating his
clothes. Oh yes, I know – you've hidden the rest.

IMM GHASSAN *opens the packet of tobacco that* ABU FIRAS *left behind. She finds a rolled cigarette in the packet, and lights it. She smokes it as she watches the light of* ABU FIRAS*'s torch get further and further away. In the distance, a radio is turned on, the faint sound of a crackly news broadcast.*

IMM GHASSAN *cries, her eyes unmoving.*

Scene Three – Meeting

Local Party Office. Night. A military boot (serving as a vase) holds a bouquet of flowers. On the wall, there is a large poster, showing a photo of a military boot, and emblazoned with the words 'We heal your wounds', the Party logo, and a photo of the leader.

ABU AL-TAYYIB *is watching a small television which faces his desk. On screen, a television report about a fall in egg production over the past year. In interviews, poultry farmers claim the reduced production is a result of the disturbing effect of the sounds of fighting. Egg producers and distributors report both a drop in the rate of egg production and a decrease in average egg size. Some farmers fail to understand why chickens are not laying as many eggs. Other farmers are not experiencing the problem at all. The local variety of chickens is laying more eggs than usual, thanks to the state's ongoing concern for them. Egg prices have risen, and citizens find themselves unable to afford a full box of eggs.*

Enter IMM AL-TAYYIB. *Her long dark hair is loose. She picks up the flowers in the vase, trims the ends of the stems, wipes the boot, and reties the laces.*

IMM AL-TAYYIB. They can't keep taking from people, and giving nothing in return.

ABU AL-TAYYIB. Every citizen gets their fair share of eggs.

IMM AL-TAYYIB. I mean what happened today.

> ABU AL-TAYYIB *ignores her comment. Quiet knocks at the door.* IMM AL-TAYYIB *goes out.* ABU KARIM *comes in.*

ABU KARIM. I thought I'd come before the others got here.

> ABU AL-TAYYIB *nods.*

> Comrade, as you asked, I have drafted two official statements. What's the next step?

ABU AL-TAYYIB. From the information we have so far, I'm going to need you to –

> ABU AL-TAYYIB *is interrupted by the sound of a heated debate taking place outside. The* MEN *of the village file in one after the other. They angrily salute, then take their places. Everyone looks serious.* ABU AL-TAYYIB *turns off the television.* ABU LU'AY *violently drags one empty chair away from the table.*

ABU KARIM. Comrades, you're early!

MEN (*muttering and looking unhappy*). Hello… Hi… Have you heard what happened to Imm Nabil's grandson… Hello…

ABU AL-TAYYIB. Comrades, shall we say the pledge?

> *All stand, silently and respectfully, and inaudibly intone the pledge. They sit.*

> Good evening, comrades, how are we all? On the agenda today we have a number of important items. (*To* ABU KARIM.) Don't we, comrade?

ABU KARIM. We do indeed, Comrade Abu al-Tayyib. First, any outstanding business? No? Then we'll move on to the agenda.

> ABU AL-TAYYIB *gestures agreement.* ABU KARIM *reads from the agenda.*

'Nominate organiser for the spontaneous demonstration on Sunday.' We need someone to organise it.

ABU AHMAD (*irritated*). Comrade Abu Ramez was put forward, but he's in hospital. He cut his thumb to vote with his blood. Then his thumb got infected.

ABU AL-TAYYIB. We wish him a speedy recovery. We'll send a delegation to see him tomorrow. Have the radio cover it, no need for TV.

ABU KARIM (*reading*). 'Second, Comrade Imm Salma to be instructed to nominate herself for election.' Remember to inform her.

ABU SALMA. She is not available for election. She's going to be pregnant.

ABU AL-TAYYIB. Abu Salma, you can postpone a pregnancy, you can't postpone an election.

ABU KARIM (*reading*). 'Third, the campaign for' –

ABU LU'AY (*angrily*). Let's get to the point. (*To the others.*) We discussed this.

ABU AL-REEM. You're right…

ABU RAMI (*looking at* ABU AL-TAYYIB). First of all, let's hear what the leadership has to say!

ABU MUHAMMAD 1. What happened today is an outrage.

ABU AHMAD (*to* ABU AL-TAYYIB). What are we going to do about Abu Firas?

ABU LU'AY. We must do something. We're angry.

ABU MUHAMMAD 2. Damn right we are.

ABU JAMAL. It's criminal!

ABU AL-REEM. I've written a report on what that ungrateful bastard has done to this village, and –

ABU LU'AY. I'll withdraw from this meeting unless we severely punish that traitor.

ABU SALMA. Calm down, comrades. We mustn't create more problems.

ABU LU'AY. Don't change your mind now. You are so slippery.

ABU SALMA. Me?

ABU MUHAMMAD 2. Slippery, just the word.

ABU SALMA. I'll ignore that. The Party needs to stand together. (*To* ABU LU'AY.) Later on, you and I are going to have words.

ABU MUHAMMAD 1. I've called my senior contacts. I informed them about Abu Firas, in case someone else tells them first. Otherwise they might think we agree with him.

ABU KARIM. They already know everything.

ABU MUHAMMAD 1. They do. But they don't have time for details.

ABU AHMAD. Comrade Abu al-Tayyib, you spoke to Abu Firas. Did you promise him anything?

ABU KARIM. Of course he didn't.

ABU MUHAMMAD 2. No way.

ABU AL-REEM. We need to circulate a petition. I prepared one at home and got the rest of the building and my family to sign it.

ABU KARIM. Comrade, petitions aren't Party protocol.

ABU ALA'. Only the opposition writes petitions, because they don't know what they're doing. But we do.

ABU SALMA. We're getting ahead of ourselves here.

ABU RAMI. How do you mean?

ABU SALMA. I just think, we're moving quite fast.

ABU MUHAMMAD 2. Sure.

ABU JAMAL. I don't mind either way.

ABU MUHAMMAD 1. Not a word from you!

ABU RAMI. Why don't you let him speak?

ABU MUHAMMAD 1. Abu Jamal has no right to comment, ever since he sold the roof to Abu Samer.

ABU JAMAL. You –

ABU ALA'. This is getting out of hand. I say, we need to bring in the security forces.

ABU JAMAL. Thank you. You're absolutely –

ABU ALA'. I'm not talking about you two!

ABU JAMAL. It's not about the roof. He just can't stand different opinions.

ABU MUHAMMAD 1. Like you even have an opinion.

ABU JAMAL. Comrade Abu al-Tayyib, are we allowed to punch people?

ABU AL-REEM. We should take Abu Firas to court. He insulted the armed forces. My cousin's husband, he's a big lawyer. I called him. He was at the gym when I called, but he's going to ring me back.

ABU AHMAD (*under his breath*). When has your 'big lawyer' ever answered you?

ABU AL-REEM. Abu Ahmad, I heard that.

ABU LU'AY. Abu Firas insulted the martyrs. That means he insulted the army. No matter who he is, that's a line you never cross.

ABU MUHAMMAD 2. Absolutely. A red line.

ABU ALA'. And he personally accused Comrade Abu al-Tayyib.

ABU AL-REEM. We should sue him for slander, that would be a lesson.

ABU RAMI (*sarcastically*). Oh yes, slander – that's defamation! Perfect for a big lawyer. Don't you have a cousin whose husband is an important lawyer?

ABU AL-REEM. Are you taking the piss?

ABU RAMI. Maybe we should have opened the coffin. That would have shut him up.

ABU JAMAL. I'm not sure. I think there's two ways of looking at it…

ABU MUHAMMAD 1. Thanks, what a useful contribution!

ABU KARIM (*interrupting*). The coffins are already sealed when they arrive at the hospital. I know, I can tell you – it is hard to reopen a coffin.

ABU ALA'. My brother works in TV. I've already spoken to him, they're doing a news item. He asked what they should call it, 'Snake in the Grass' or 'Back-Stabber Attacks'?

ABU JAMAL. Comrade Abu al-Tayyib, can I go to the loo?

ABU AL-TAYYIB. Well, I'm so glad you all thought to ask my opinion. (*Uncomfortable silence.*) Have we finished? Do you have any more 'genius ideas'?

ABU AHMAD. Comrade Abu al-Tayyib. It sounds like there's a plan in place. Are there orders from above?

ABU AL-TAYYIB. Are you in any doubt about that?

ABU MUHAMMAD 2. No, of course not.

ABU MUHAMMAD 1. We had a meeting before this meeting.

ABU AL-TAYYIB *is displeased at this. He looks accusingly at* ABU KARIM *for failing to tell him about it. The others realise he shouldn't have mentioned it.*

Abu Lu'ay was saying that Abu Firas is a real danger to the village…

ABU KARIM. Comrade…

ABU AHMAD. Comrade, it wasn't really a meeting. We just sort of, you know, got together on our way here.

ABU MUHAMMAD 1. Abu Firas is inventing all kinds of stories. He called me earlier. I didn't answer of course. But Abu Samer picked up. 'What did your boy say when he called from the front?' He's asking everyone. He even thinks the boys tell their parents about Firas! His own son! He's really lost it.

ABU MUHAMMAD 2. Lost it completely.

ABU AL-TAYYIB. These phone calls, why are you so worked up? Please tell your sons to stop calling. Keep their minds on the battle.

ABU MUHAMMAD 1. Abu Ala', when your son called you, how many had he captured?

ABU ALA'. More than five. How about yours?

ABU MUHAMMAD 2. Impressive!

ABU RAMI. He hasn't called me. Probably doesn't have any credit.

ABU AHMAD. Our schoolteacher Abu Firas is polluting the minds of our children.

ABU ALA'. Yes, we need to tell our kids to stay away from him.

ABU LU'AY. We need to isolate him, until the government can punish him. Every person, every house, every village – they are all a miniature version of the state. We must help the government stop the contagion.

ABU AL-TAYYIB. Comrade Abu Lu'ay, are you telling me how to do my job?

ABU LU'AY. No, of course not.

ABU AL-TAYYIB. We will deal with Abu Firas at the appropriate time.

ABU JAMAL (*still concerned about going to the bathroom*). Sorry but, you know, are we going to be long?

ABU ALA'. It would reassure people to arrest Abu Firas. And remind them that a betrayal is always punished. We can't leave him on the loose, the bastard.

ABU AL-TAYYIB. That 'bastard' has relatives in high places. He has connections. Now, we've discussed this enough.

ABU LU'AY. We can't sweep this under the carpet. Otherwise we'll have to pull out of this meeting.

ABU AL-TAYYIB. Oh, so you've planned a mutiny? Abu Lu'ay, I'll ignore that. Or there'll be trouble, and you know what that means.

ABU MUHAMMAD 2. I do.

ABU MUHAMMAD 1. Yes, when did we start tolerating different opinions?

ABU AL-TAYYIB. Abu Muhammad, the Party elite has a lot of respect for Abu Firas.

ABU MUHAMMAD 2. Yes, I know that.

    ABU MUHAMMAD 1 *mutters inaudibly*.

ABU AL-TAYYIB. Let's not hear the phrase 'different opinions' uttered here again.

    Loud banging at the door. All immediately pay attention.

ABU FIRAS (*from outside*). Open the door! Open up, Abu al-Tayyib, I know you are having a meeting. Let me in! You can't get away from me, I won't let you. Come on, you cowards, open up!

    ABU KARIM *angrily makes a move to get up*.
    ABU AL-TAYYIB *stops him with a warning glance*.

ABU LU'AY. Filthy traitor! No way. Get out of here!

ABU ALA'. How does he dare? He thinks he can just turn up at our meeting?

ABU AHMAD. I say we confront him.

ABU MUHAMMAD 1. That traitor is not coming in here and dirtying the party offices.

ABU ALA'. I will kill him.

ABU MUHAMMAD 2. Me too.

ABU FIRAS (*from outside*). Don't hide, if you are men. Let me in! Abu al-Tayyib, open the door! You cowards... Let me in!

MEN. Get out of here! You're not one of us. You have no right to be here. Traitor!

The banging at the door gets louder and tension increases.
ABU AL-TAYYIB *allows the clamour to continue until everyone is uncomfortable. He quietly makes a call on his mobile.*

ABU AL-TAYYIB (*indicating his phone*). You need to realise that, with a real emergency, the government is there when you need it. Unless you want him knocking on your doors one by one.

ABU FIRAS*'s voice gets quieter. It sounds as if he was pulled away from the door by force.*

Now listen – enough bright ideas. I've been in touch with my colleagues at the highest levels. Their response is that we should take it easy. It's not clear if Abu Firas is in a fit state of mind. We need to limit the damage.

ABU SALMA. Well said.

ABU AHMAD. How come the government failed to see what was happening to Abu Firas?

ABU RAMI. It is a bit odd.

ABU AHMAD. I mean, we have satellite surveillance that can pinpoint someone in a field fucking their goat. Excuse me. But then we have no idea what's going on in the head of one of our own Party members.

ABU ALA' (*hissing*). Shut up! They might be recording this meeting, and then we're in deep shit!

ABU AL-TAYYIB. Naturally, Abu Firas's behaviour wasn't a surprise to me. Have faith. This incident won't be passed over in silence. But be patient. We need to behave respectfully towards our elders. That man used to have a seat at this table. If anything, we want him to come back to the fold.

ABU MUHAMMAD 2. Wise words.

ABU JAMAL. Honestly, I can't wait any longer.

ABU AL-TAYYIB. You'll have to. The decision has been made, right at the top.

ABU JAMAL (*finally getting up to go to the toilet*). Well I need to make a decision down below!

ABU AL-TAYYIB *gestures in exasperation. Some of the* MEN *laugh*.

ABU AL-TAYYIB. If one person failed to behave properly, it is our Sheikh. He has been so passive.

SHEIKH. Comrade Abu al-Tayyib, permit me to defend myself. Since it happened, you have not let me speak.

ABU AL-TAYYIB. And I still will not let you speak. You need to listen. The time for you to speak will come later – to the people whose faith and trust has been shaken. 'The martyr belongs to his nation!' What does that mean, Sheikh? A soldier doesn't sacrifice himself for Mummy and Daddy and the living room! The Holy Qur'an and the Hadith declare a martyr must be buried where he falls – and not lie around waiting for a visit from his family.

SHEIKH. You are quite right.

ABU AL-TAYYIB. Comrade Abu Salam, my dear Sheikh. I do not need to tell you how to do your job. At the funeral, one word from you would have been enough to bury this matter. You need to reassure people about the fate of their children.

SHEIKH. Of course, they do –

ABU AL-TAYYIB. Next time, I won't turn a blind eye, it will go on your file.

The SHEIKH *understands what* ABU AL-TAYYIB *means.* ABU JAMAL *comes back from the bathroom, some of the* MEN *grin.*

ABU JAMAL. Have I missed anything?

ABU MUHAMMAD 1. You've lost weight!

Stifled sniggers.

ABU MUHAMMAD 2 (*quietly, gloating*). He put Abu Salam in his place. You missed that!

ABU AL-TAYYIB *takes a piece of paper out of his pocket.*
ABU AL-TAYYIB *and* ABU KARIM *exchange meaningful glances.*

ABU AL-TAYYIB. We have received the official statement from the executive committee. Let me read it to you.

ABU KARIM (*in evident collusion*). Please go ahead, comrade!

ABU AL-TAYYIB (*reading*). 'Our nation has led the way, first, in recognising the role of the martyr in society, and second, in offering assistance to the families of martyrs. On this occasion, we are happy to announce news of a generous initiative, signed into effect by the executive committee. A mountain goat for the family of each martyr. A goat for every family that has given the greatest gift it possessed.' (*Puts down the piece of paper.*) The income from the goat will help each family be self-sufficient. You see, the government stands with us in our time of need.

ABU MUHAMMAD 2. Is it one goat per family, or one goat per martyr?

ABU AHMAD. Where is Abu Firas? He should hear this!

ABU RAMI. Dear God, this is too generous! We don't need a thing. We're poor, it's true. But, at a time like this, we don't want to be a burden to our nation. Surely, there must be people in worse need than us.

ABU ALA' (*interrupting*). Just the other day I was saying to Imm Ala', we can't afford – (*He is so moved he can't contain himself, and bursts into tears.*)

ABU JAMAL. It's okay, Abu Ala', it's okay. See, the worst is over now.

ABU RAMI. Thank you so much, Abu al-Tayyib. Thanks to the general secretary, and thanks to everyone who contributed – and everyone who understood our pain and need.

ABU MUHAMMAD 1 (*addressing* ABU JAMAL). Where you going to put your goat now, smart arse? You shouldn't have sold that roof, should you?

ABU AL-TAYYIB. Let me finish so you can hear the full plan. (*Resumes reading from the piece of paper.*) 'A special committee has been appointed to identify families who deserve to benefit from the scheme. They will examine every family's record and degree of sacrifice. We urge all citizens to register.'

Hubbub and excitement. ABU AL-TAYYIB *folds up the paper.* ABU AL-TAYYIB *passes an envelope to* ABU RAMI, *who distributes forms to those present.* IMM AL-TAYYIB *sticks her head around the door to remind* ABU AL-TAYYIB *of the time.*

And now let us wrap up our meeting. It is time for the women's mosaic class.

The telephone rings and ABU AL-TAYYIB *answers.*

Yes... Yes... Okay, you get back to it. We will have reinforcements with you right away! (*Hangs up.*) Abu Firas is at the hospital again, making a scene. He is trying to find Firas's body. They are telling me he has smashed the windows and he is trying to break down the doors. Abu Karim, say the pledge, then get down there ASAP to deal with the situation. We will send you some back-ups.

ABU AL-TAYYIB *stands up. The others follow suit and intone the pledge.* ABU KARIM *leaves in a hurry and the others follow.*

ABU AL-TAYYIB *is left alone.* IMM AL-TAYYIB *enters and regards* ABU AL-TAYYIB. ABU AL-TAYYIB *leaves and* IMM AL-TAYYIB *follows him.*

ZAHRA *enters, she is alone in the room. She surveys the chairs and the chaos, then sits down at the head of the table.*

Scene Four – Who is he?

A viewpoint overlooking the town. Next to the statue of The Hero. Night-time.

ABU FIRAS *sits looking out over the hospital and the cemetery. Some time goes by, then* FADI, JUDE *and* MUDAR *appear.* MUDAR *is carrying an M16 rifle.* ABU FIRAS *leaps up in relief. The three boys look awkward.*

ABU FIRAS. I knew you wouldn't leave me by myself.

FADI. Sir, God rest his soul.

ABU FIRAS. Why did you let Firas go?

FADI. We had no idea that you didn't know.

JUDE. It's a great honour –

MUDAR (*to* JUDE *and* FADI). We agreed not to –

ABU FIRAS (*interrupting*). But you, you're young, nothing is worth dying for.

JUDE. That's not what you used to tell us. (*As if repeating a lesson from memory.*) 'Honour, nation, sacrifice, principles, dignity, fraternity… Turn to page fifty-six… Look at diagram three…'

FADI. Sir, you're really pale. You need to get some sleep.

JUDE (*in a whisper*). Yeah, then we can enjoy ourselves…

FADI (*to* JUDE). Shut up, he'll hear you!

ABU FIRAS. The coffin was too short for him.

JUDE. He keeps teaching us stuff that's the exact opposite of the last thing we learnt. How am I supposed to know which one is right?

ABU FIRAS. Did Firas tell you he was going? What do you know?

MUDAR. He never said anything…

ABU FIRAS. Did he want to join the army?

MUDAR. Firas! Sir, he loved weapons, more than any of us.

ABU FIRAS. Firas? How come? Why did he go? And why have you got that gun with you?

JUDE. He's your son, sir.

MUDAR. Don't let him drag you into it, man.

FADI. Sir, he went to defend the nation. Against terrorists. Against terrorists who want to destroy the safety and security of our country. They want to kill us all! One look at what's written on your ID card, and they chop off your head and play football with it.

MUDAR. Great, now you've got him started.

ABU FIRAS. The nation needs you alive, not dead! Firas's death won't change anything. Think about it! You're not even seventeen. What does this war have to do with you? Or with Firas? What are you fighting for? Do you have any idea what's happening out there, who's killing who, and why? Do you?

FADI. Don't worry, sir, we've all got 3G.

JUDE. We're fighting this war so there won't be any more wars!

ABU FIRAS. Who's filling your head with this nonsense? Does no one around here want to use their brain for half a minute? Do you memorise whatever they feed you? They are using you to fight their battles. They're killing you. And no one is asking any questions. Your friend died, surrounded and afraid. God knows, they probably never sent anyone to rescue him. His voice was shaking. I'll never forgive them. Firas was murdered. I'm not moving from here. There's the hospital, there's the cemetery, and here's me.

JUDE (*whispering to* MUDAR). Do we ever get a break from his lectures?

MUDAR. But what's that got to do with us? And what's it got to do with seeing Firas?

FADI. Sir, 'surrounded'? When he rang you, did he tell you he was surrounded?

JUDE (*doubtfully*). It's bullshit... Those calls, that's not what the other boys were saying!

MUDAR. I'm heading off. I don't want anyone to see us.

ABU FIRAS. So, what do the boys say when they call their families?

MUDAR. We don't know anything about it.

FADI. Ask someone else, sir.

ABU FIRAS. Why won't you tell me?

MUDAR. We don't know.

ABU FIRAS. Why?

MUDAR. We just don't.

JUDE. He is scared of his dad. Abu al-Tayyib always finds out about everything.

MUDAR (*to JUDE, under his breath*). Fuck off.

JUDE. Fuck you too. Everyone knows. All the guys ring their families. Like you wouldn't ring up your dad, straight away, to brag about how many people you'd killed!

MUDAR. Mind your own business.

JUDE. Oh, come off it! You'd be like, 'I've captured ten people and killed them.' When actually you were hiding in a bunker. (*Indicating* FADI.) His dumbass brother called, he was shitting himself. The only one to admit it.

FADI (*to JUDE*). Shut your face, dickhead!

ABU FIRAS. Your brother was scared?

MUDAR. Right, I'm off.

ABU FIRAS. Answer me!

FADI. I didn't really get what he was saying. Anyway, he only spoke to my mum.

ABU FIRAS. What did he say to her?

MUDAR (*moving away*). I'm going to go and stand over there.

FADI. He said to Mum, he'd caught some terrorists, he didn't know what to do with them. Whatever, it doesn't matter.

ABU FIRAS. Where is your brother now?

JUDE. That whole family's soft...

FADI shoves JUDE.

ABU FIRAS. Stop it, you two!

They stop.

Carry on!

FADI. That's it.

ABU FIRAS. You didn't find out why he was scared?

JUDE (*pointing at* FADI). It's him that's scared. The guys call to share their good news and make their families feel proud.

MUDAR. He's making it up, sir – he lies all the time. His brother is a hero. A martyr. My dad was really proud of him.

ABU FIRAS. Let him finish. He can speak for himself.

JUDE. He's full of shit!

ABU FIRAS. He's the only one of you that isn't! I want to know what happened to his brother and to Firas!

JUDE. No offence, sir, but even you're a bit full of –

ABU FIRAS *slaps* JUDE. JUDE *lunges at* ABU FIRAS. MUDAR *and* FADI *restrain him.*

ABU FIRAS. How dare you! Get the hell out of here, the lot of you.

JUDE (*the others prevent his words from being fully heard by* ABU FIRAS). He's fucking mad! We didn't come here to see you, we're on duty here. We've been told to keep away from you.

MUDAR. Come on, stop it!

FADI. You were asking for it anyway. (*To* ABU FIRAS.) Please, sir, I really think you should go. I swear, they're not going to move Firas from the hospital. We can see the whole

town from here, anyway. We're staying up late because
we're on duty tonight. We can call you if anything happens.

MUDAR. I'm not calling anyone.

ABU FIRAS (*to* JUDE). Go and put some cold water on his face.

ABU FIRAS *grips* FADI*'s shoulder, as if he is entrusting
him with his son Firas.* ABU FIRAS *rises and leaves.*

JUDE. Fucking twat! Every time something happens, he takes it
out on us.

FADI. It's hardly the first time he's hit you, what's the big deal?

JUDE. If I get hold of him, I'll knock him out.

MUDAR. Calm down.

FADI *whistles.*

SAMI *appears, he sticks out his head, peering around to
check* ABU FIRAS *has gone.*

SAMI. Has he fucked off yet?

FADI. He's heading down to the hospital, see.

JUDE (*to* SAMI). You can suck my dick, you –

MUDAR *puts his hand over* JUDE*'s mouth.*

MUDAR. What if someone's watching! Keep it down.

JUDE (*muffled*). I got a slap in the face, waiting for you, all
because of your hash.

SAMI. *My* hash! Fuck you, go and get it yourself next time!

MUDAR. Did you get it?

SAMI. We nearly got caught. What are the fucking chances?
Abu Firas broke all the windows. Officials turned up, wanted
to search everyone. I don't know how I got out.

MUDAR. We can talk about that later.

SAMI. I'm still shaking, I can't even stand up properly.

FADI. Show us how much you got!

JUDE. Did you get any pills?

FADI. Did you see Firas's coffin?

SAMI. Dude, I was terrified, fuck, it was like… I saw God.

FADI (*genuinely affected*). I can't believe Firas is dead…

MUDAR. Shhhhhh. (*To* SAMI.) You should've seen how shithead here was talking to Sir.

JUDE. 'Sir', my arse! The way he treats us.

SAMI. I don't believe it.

  SAMI *hands out a joint, which they light and pass round.*

FADI. Why have they got us guarding the statue?

MUDAR. It's until they set up a proper security thing for it.

FADI. For the statue?

MUDAR. You know, so it doesn't get nicked or smashed up or pissed on before the ceremony.

JUDE. When's that then?

MUDAR. I dunno! Whatever. Shut up, and get on with guarding.

JUDE. What would be the point of that?

FADI. I can't really see anyone bothering, to be honest.

MUDAR. You never know.

JUDE. Maybe the stray dogs…

MUDAR. Yeah! Have you seen them the last few nights?

FADI. How come?

JUDE. How come what?

MUDAR. There's more than usual.

SAMI (*to* FADI). It's the army uniform, they've put it on the statue.

JUDE. It's still got blood on it, see!

FADI. So, it's the blood. (*Thinks*.) There's dead bodies all over the place. That's why there's been so many dogs recently.

JUDE *suddenly yelps in terror and* FADI *jumps up in fright. The others laugh.*

Scene Five – Confrontation

The school. Children can be heard playing football outside in the playground.

ABU FIRAS *opens the door, enters the classroom, wipes the blackboard. He writes on the board: 'PERIOD 1. SUBJECT: History. TOPIC: Independence Revolts against the Ottoman Empire.'* ABU FIRAS *checks his watch. The bell rings to announce the start of classes. He sits down at his desk, angry at the students' tardiness. He looks towards the window. The door opens and* ABU AL-TAYYIB *enters.* ABU FIRAS *is surprised.*

ABU AL-TAYYIB. Good morning!

ABU FIRAS. You. So, you've followed me here?

ABU AL-TAYYIB. The school belongs to us all.

ABU FIRAS. I want to give you a slap.

ABU AL-TAYYIB. Well, of course, from our respected teacher, I would accept that... After all, it would not be the first time.

ABU FIRAS *gestures at him to leave.*

Do you expect to stay on at the school? You are lucky we did not arrest you, or break your legs.

ABU FIRAS. Get out!

ABU AL-TAYYIB. I do not want to be disrespectful. But you make it, well – unavoidable. Abu Firas, it is time we let you take a break. Over the years, you have taught almost everyone in the village... Now it is time for you to enjoy the gratitude and the reward that you deserve. So, if anyone's going to get out, then it's you.

ABU FIRAS *gets up to leave, furious.*

Hold on, not straight away! I wish I could let you do whatever you want. After all, in the past, none of us dared to raise our voice at you.

ABU FIRAS. I would have cut out your tongue.

ABU AL-TAYYIB. Let us talk, respectfully, like teacher and student.

ABU AL-TAYYIB *gestures to* ABU FIRAS *to sit down.*
ABU FIRAS *remains standing.* ABU AL-TAYYIB *sits down on one of the classroom desks.*

I should not need to say this to an intelligent person like you, Abu Firas. What you have done is heresy. You know that. You were brought up to know that. Out of all of us, you know best when a child should not talk back to its father. When it's okay to cry, and when it is not. When we are allowed to have a new cowboy costume, or just wear the same summer clothes, even in winter, without complaining. But now you have put me in this predicament.

ABU FIRAS. You put yourself in it.

ABU AL-TAYYIB. Wrong. You embarrassed me. And I cannot believe you embarrassed me in front of them. Telling everyone, 'Abu al-Tayyib promised to let me see the body of my son. And he did not keep his promise.'

ABU FIRAS. It's true!

ABU AL-TAYYIB. And since when do we tell the truth? Huh? Tell me. Please. In this classroom, right here. Since I was fifteen, sixteen. Has anyone ever told the truth? Has anyone ever demanded it? Does anyone want it? Does anyone even need it? What is the truth, Abu Firas? That I did not let you see your son?

ABU FIRAS. The truth is – *why* you didn't let me see my son.

ABU AL-TAYYIB *gives a mocking smile.*

ABU AL-TAYYIB. Of course. Son of a big shot. Grandson of another big shot. Educated, cultured. You always had a TV, even as a kid, and a washing machine, and a car. Your father made sure never to hit us when you were visiting the barracks. Because you were so delicate. (*Pause.*) Abu Firas... Enough! We all know you failed to do military service. Do you know what the body of a martyr looks like? When an RPG hits a tank, what happens inside? The soldier melts. His body fuses with the tank, and ends up in a lump of stinking metal that you cannot prise apart. Our boys are coming back in pieces. Legs and kidneys. And a finger that says, 'Bugger you!' – like this! (*Points one finger.*) Can you imagine what that is like? Abu Firas, do you want the families to see their boys like that?

ABU FIRAS. They have the right. Who are you to decide for them?

ABU AL-TAYYIB. But now you're scared. You do not think about any of this. Your performance at the funeral was a disgrace. Families were holding a picture of their son on his wedding night. They do not want to see him as a lump of rotten flesh.

ABU FIRAS *remains silent.*

After seeing something so terrible, no parent would let their son fight. Do you want to leave the village to the enemy?

ABU FIRAS. Who are *you* leaving the village to? Soon there will be no one left. Tell me, none of the boys come back wounded. Why is that? They are all dead.

ABU AL-TAYYIB *is silent.*

Good, that means it is my turn to speak! You are happy that your people are all over the TV, showing off our dead children and celebrating. You tell everyone you are fighting terrorism, and winning? Look me in the eye! Tell me that people really think we are winning. Do you really believe that?

ABU AL-TAYYIB. I believe it.

ABU FIRAS. Abu al-Tayyib, you are playing with the lives of our sons. Why don't you go and fight? Shame!

ABU AL-TAYYIB *is about to speak, but* ABU FIRAS *interrupts him.*

I know why you are here. You are scared. You are scared of me. Why? Because now I have nothing left to lose. In a country like this, that is the most dangerous thing. (*Thinks.*) My son and I never knew each other. I fooled myself into thinking, 'Surely Firas knows – we are doing this to keep him safe. Telling him everything would be like pushing him into prison with my own hands. He's too young to be a hypocrite.' We both kept quiet. And now, suddenly, I realise he actually believed it all, and he refused to believe anything else. Do you want us to keep doing that to our children? Firas, al-Tayyib, Kinan – and Mudar? Your boys are still alive. Go on, send them abroad! Do not waste your time talking to me! I have had enough.

ABU AL-TAYYIB (*agitated, raising his voice to drown out* ABU FIRAS). This is a war, not a game. Young men are dying, so that you and I can stay alive. You are feeling crushed, because of your son.

ABU FIRAS. Yes, I wish I could go back in time. Tell me. How did Firas die?

ABU AL-TAYYIB. Your son died a martyr. He did his duty. Those young men have fought, and laid down their lives for us. The how, and when, and who, and what... Those are minor details. They sacrificed themselves... for us. Otherwise the enemy's children would be playing football with your head!

ABU FIRAS. Our children are slipping through our fingers. Please, for a moment, be human. No one's watching.

ABU AL-TAYYIB. Even there you're wrong. Look – we're in the middle of a war. It's either kill or be killed. The war swallows up everything that came before it. We can only see who manages to stay alive. Then it will be your job to teach, if you are still alive.

ABU FIRAS. Can you hear yourself? You are a criminal. Our children are not martyrs, they are cannon fodder.

ABU AL-TAYYIB. You cannot make people lose their faith in martyrdom. Anything, but that... That is the worst treachery you can commit. Is any boy going to sign up if his teacher is saying the war is pointless? That is criminal. The enemy will slaughter us all in our beds. Your madness is contagious. People are scared of you, scared for their children.

ABU FIRAS. That is not true.

ABU AL-TAYYIB. How would you know what is true?

ABU FIRAS. I can feel it. We started this war. And now it is crushing us underfoot like cowshit. We are the reason it happened. We invited monsters into our homes, and now we cannot get them out. The war is –

ABU AL-TAYYIB *applauds mockingly*.

ABU AL-TAYYIB. Great. I was sad for you to begin with, but now you have gone too far. You will be lucky to stay out of prison. And you definitely will not continue as a teacher. Listen. There is no such thing as a peaceful movement for regime change. You are vindictive.

ABU FIRAS. You're heartless. You just keep talking so you don't have to feel anything.

ABU AL-TAYYIB. Resign. Let us have done with this selfish nonsense.

ABU FIRAS. 'Selfish'!

ABU AL-TAYYIB. Of course. Everyone has a son at the front line. At any moment, one of us might get tragic news.

ABU FIRAS. But first, the calls – the boys phoning home.

ABU AL-TAYYIB. You want to make that a big thing?

ABU FIRAS. It is a big thing.

ABU AL-TAYYIB. No, it's a phase. Just a boys' thing that caught on, but now it is over. True, a young soldier, a boy, was unprofessional – he called his family. It should not have happened. That is all.

ABU FIRAS. They are all doing it.

ABU AL-TAYYIB. It's a serious tactical slip, I know. I'm trying to have a word about it. But there's no need for a big discussion.

ABU FIRAS. I know my son. He was scared. I need to know why he was left alone.

ABU AL-TAYYIB. I'd be surprised if he was scared. Firas was one of our brightest and best young men. But even soldiers get scared sometimes. They're only human.

ABU FIRAS. The more you talk, the more I suspect there's something going on. Otherwise it wouldn't have come to this.

ABU AL-TAYYIB. I haven't lied to you. I didn't promise you anything, you just misunderstood. There is nothing else I can do.

ABU FIRAS. Who are you trying to fool?

Pause.

ABU AL-TAYYIB. You're just having a tantrum, because you are not getting special treatment. You might be the son of someone important, but now you are like everyone else. Fine. Next time we will give you a special badge. And stop knocking on doors, saying, 'Come on, let's go and dig up the graves and see if our sons are dead!' We need to reassure people. Fortunately, the government has the matter in hand. They plan to distribute goats to the families of every martyr.

ABU FIRAS *is taken aback.*

It's time this nonsense was put to bed. We cannot have a grieving mother worrying that her son or husband is not inside their coffin.

ABU FIRAS. It's true!

ABU AL-TAYYIB. I don't give a damn about you or this truth of yours.

ABU FIRAS. And I don't give a damn about you or your goats!

ABU FIRAS *starts to leave*.

ABU AL-TAYYIB. Wait! I can have you arrested, and make an example of you. The charges are ready. For interfering in military secrets. (*Pause*.) It's that simple. Firas will have to be buried.

ABU FIRAS. The sheikhs will not allow it.

ABU AL-TAYYIB. The sheikhs will fall into line. Every last one.

ABU FIRAS *slumps defeatedly into a chair, his arms dangling limply*. ABU AL-TAYYIB *approaches him*.

Abu Firas, it is not easy for me to see you crushed. I am indebted to your father – I will be until the day I die. And I retain a lot of affection and respect for you.

ABU FIRAS (*pushing* ABU AL-TAYYIB*'s hand away in disgust*). This isn't how you show respect.

ABU AL-TAYYIB. Cooperate with us. Agree to that, and you can see your son.

ABU FIRAS *waits expectantly*.

ABU FIRAS. I don't follow.

ABU AL-TAYYIB. That doesn't matter. Either you agree, or you refuse. We can talk about the details later.

Pause.

ABU FIRAS. Never.

ABU AL-TAYYIB. Odd.

ABU FIRAS. No, I will never cooperate with you.

ABU AL-TAYYIB. As you like. (*Moves away from* ABU FIRAS.)

ABU FIRAS. Even if I did… How do I know that you will show him to me?

ABU AL-TAYYIB. Because I said so.

ABU AL-TAYYIB *heads for the door*.

Before you go, write your resignation letter. We do not want any trouble. The kids are now forbidden from coming near you. And you must stay away from them.

Pause.

ABU FIRAS. So you're going to leave them without an education?

ABU AL-TAYYIB. If one teacher goes, there are ten to replace him. History doesn't change. Nor does the curriculum. Zahra is coming to teach them. She was your student, and a good one. You taught her well. This generation needs fresh blood, someone who speaks to them in their own language. Zahra is a clever girl. Also, she is one of us. She does not keep bits of opposition propaganda – yes, I know about that.

Pause.

ABU FIRAS. I cannot cooperate with you.

ABU AL-TAYYIB *heads for the door.*

And I will not forgive you.

ABU AL-TAYYIB. Well, maybe you should thank me. (*Pausing, before he leaves*.) The boys did find your son Firas – out in the fields, without a weapon, being eaten by hyenas. I told them – never, ever breathe a word about this in the village. Firas must be remembered as a martyr.

ABU AL-TAYYIB *exits*. ABU FIRAS *is dumbstruck*.

On the wall is a large poster bearing the Party logo.
ABU FIRAS goes over to it, and pulls it down in anger and
frustration. Underneath it is the same picture. He tears
through it and underneath finds the same picture, again.
He keeps tearing and every time reveals the same picture,
until he finally arrives at an old photo of a person whose
features are unclear: the Dictator. ABU AL-TAYYIB *stands*
watching him from outside the window. Their eyes meet.

Scene Six – Nightmares

ABU FIRAS*'s humble home. Night-time. Darkness. A single candle lights the place.*

On the walls are many photos of martyrs, clippings of maps and scraps of paper covered with handwriting. The television is lying on its side on the floor, suggesting ABU FIRAS *has thrown it there. His son Firas's clothes are in the room.*

ABU FIRAS *is in bed trying to sleep. He tosses and turns. He gets up. He lights a candle and turns on the radio. The voices are crackly and distorted, and he switches it off. He takes out his tobacco and rolls a cigarette which he smokes slowly. He extinguishes the candle and gets back into bed. The sound of crying can be heard from the bed. Darkness.*

The sound of dogs barking. ABU FIRAS *is trapped in a telephone box in which the phone has no handset, and trying unsuccessfully to get out. The barking sounds frightening, as if the dogs are lying in wait for him outside.* ABU FIRAS *manages to get the door open and set off at a run in an attempt to escape the dogs. He continues to run. Darkness.*

ABU FIRAS, *in bed, wakes from his nightmare, panting and in a panic, and rubs his face. Strange sounds and movements.* ABU FIRAS *looks around. There's nothing there. He remains sitting up.*

A goat approaches the bed. It is wearing glasses. It looks at ABU FIRAS. ABU FIRAS *lights the lamp by his bed and sees the goat. He isn't scared. He watches it. It comes closer.*

VOICE OF IMM FIRAS (*quietly*). Firas is dead.

ABU FIRAS. No, he's not.

VOICE OF IMM FIRAS. He's not eating.

ABU FIRAS. He's moving his eyes.

VOICE OF IMM FIRAS. He isn't.

ABU FIRAS. He's looking at me.

VOICE OF IMM FIRAS. He's not moving.

ABU FIRAS. He doesn't like meat.

VOICE OF IMM FIRAS. You cooked it.

ABU FIRAS. Every time you say this, in the end – it turns out
he's not dead. We go to the graveyard, he's not there, we
come home. Then we go again.

VOICE OF IMM FIRAS. Shall we buy him a rope, so we don't
have to keep going back and forth?

ABU FIRAS. I don't know.

VOICE OF IMM FIRAS. Why did you let him die without
washing his hands?

Lights down. ABU FIRAS *screams. He wakes up to find the
goat has gone. He sits up on the edge of the bed. He lights
the candle. He sits next to the telephone. He thinks. He blows
out the candle. Darkness.*

ABU FIRAS *picks up the handset and dials a number.*

VOICE OF ABU AL-TAYYIB. Hello?

ABU FIRAS. What do I have to do?

VOICE OF ABU AL-TAYYIB. Ah, you have been persuaded.

ABU FIRAS. I want to see my son.

VOICE OF ABU AL-TAYYIB. Very well. Miss Hayam Abbas,
from the TV station, is ready to come over with a
cameraman. Follow her instructions.

ABU FIRAS. And what about Firas?

VOICE OF ABU AL-TAYYIB. You will find out.

The electricity comes back on.

ABU FIRAS *is left holding the receiver after* ABU
AL-TAYYIB *hangs up. He drops it suddenly, as if he
has made a big mistake.*

Scene Seven – Everything is all right

Town square. Middle of the day. The VILLAGERS *are all
gathered in the square, apart from* ABU FIRAS *and* IMM
GHASSAN. ABU AL-TAYYIB's BODYGUARDS. TV CREW.
*A large number of goats, eating bits of paper which are lying on
the floor. There are more goats than there are men. Colourful
flags are being waved, including a FC Barcelona flag. The
bleating of goats makes it hard to hear much of what is
happening. On screen is a news item about the merits of goats.
Colours on screen are much brighter than those on the stage.*

ABU RAMI. The leadership is so clever. Goats are the only
creatures who eat everything. Grass. Wood. Sand. Paper.
Wire, even plastic! Anything they find in their path. We don't
even need to worry about feeding them.

The TECHNICIAN *gestures to* VILLAGERS *to move
together, so the screen shows heaving crowds.*

PRESENTER (*on screen and on stage*). We are here today
because of our martyrs and their sacrifices. Without the brave
martyrs, this village would have been wiped off the map.
Our martyrs are the soaring eagles of earth and sky. When
we hear the roar of their fighter jets, we know the enemy is
about to be crushed. Our martyrs are blooming fruits of
goodness and generosity. (*Pause.*) We are gathered here
today to show our faith in the noble value of martyrdom.
To show our appreciation of the families who bear the loss of
their sons and husbands. These mothers and these wives
dedicate their life to raising a hero – a hero imbued with love
for their nation, love for its soil. (*Pause.*) Today, we are
delighted to announce that the martyrs' families are to
receive a goat to show them that the nation has not forgotten
them. The goat reminds them of the son they have lost, or
husband, or father. What a heart-warming sight to see the
village full of goats.

The PRESENTER (*on screen and on stage*) *interviews*
IMM NABIL. *The* PRESENTER *is holding* (*out of sight
of the camera*) *a piece of paper for* IMM NABIL *to read
her answers.*

Today's news is moving and poignant. Every family, so proud to have a martyr, will receive a mountain goat. (*Addressed to* IMM NABIL.) Imm Nabil, kindly tell us how you feel, hearing this announcement.

IMM NABIL. Honestly, I do not know what to say. I could sing you a song.

IMM NABIL *sings, her face expressionless.*[2]

My country, O my country,
Take my firstborn son
You're the guardians of the homeland
You've tread the paths of my ancestors
Love, O my country
Take my firstborn son
The swing you love, son, was made by our country
And your books and your pens and your bread too
In this land I raised you
And to it I've dedicated you
I urge you to love it
Grow up and do your duty by it
You'll be the guardian of the homeland
You'll tread the paths of my ancestors
Love, O my country
Take my firstborn son.

PRESENTER (*on screen and on stage*). Oh, that was lovely. Thank you so much, Imm Nabil. Now, can you tell us a little about the spontaneous gathering that is taking place here today?

IMM NABIL *nods in assent. The* CAMERAMAN *continues filming her in close-up, then films the goats and the* VILLAGERS *interacting with them. Some are taking selfies with the goats, others are trying to pick which goat they are going to take.*

(*On screen and on stage.*) So, Imm Nabil, this morning there was a magnificent funeral. You said goodbye to your grandson Yazan. Can you tell us a little bit about how that made you feel?

---

2. A translation, with some modifications for the purposes of the production, of 'Ya Biladi Khudi Shadi' by 'Isa Ayyub (1946–2002).

IMM NABIL *is silent.*

(*On screen.*) Did you bid farewell to him before he was buried?

IMM NABIL *is silent.*

(*On stage, speaking to* IMM NABIL.) Why aren't you saying anything? The answers are right here!

IMM NABIL. I can't see.

PRESENTER (*on stage*). What? Why didn't you say so?

VILLAGER (*muttering*). Excuse me, madam. Imm Nabil can't see. She is nearly blind.

IMM NABIL *remains silent.*

PRESENTER (*on stage*). Oh, no need to talk. If you like, you can ululate instead. Or maybe recite some of his favourite poetry.

On screen, close-ups of the goats.

IMM NABIL (*on stage*). Oh, if only you knew. When I'm alone, I cry and cry. I mean, we'd unpacked all his boxes, and we dusted all his books. I bought him a lamp, so he can study at night. He's been saying for a year he needs a lamp. He wanted to be an engineer. Do you want to film his desk?

PRESENTER (*on stage*). The boy's father, your son Nabil, is away fighting now. Would you like to talk about him?

IMM NABIL (*on stage*). Oh, is he watching us now, from the front line?

PRESENTER (*on stage and on screen*). God willing, yes, he's watching. Go ahead.

IMM NABIL. I'd like to thank Mr President… And the army… Abu al-Tayyib… And you… Everybody… (*Lying.*) Please tell Nabil, your son Yazan is doing fine. (*Bursts into tears.*)

PRESENTER (*on screen*). Those must be tears of joy.

IMM NABIL (*on screen*). Yes, they must be.

> ABU AL-TAYYIB *arrives. The crowd clears a path for him. Applause.*

> *On screen, the camera follows* ABU AL-TAYYIB, *accompanied by uplifting music, and shots of the* VILLAGERS *welcoming him.* ABU AL-TAYYIB *salutes villagers, then pats goats on the head. A goat pursues* IMM RAMI, *who runs away in fright. One of the* MEN *sets upon the goat, brandishing a large stick, to stop it following* IMM RAMI. *The* BODYGUARDS *hurry over to stop him beating it. It is impossible to control the goats in a civilised fashion.*

> *The* PRESENTER (*on stage*) *salutes* ABU AL-TAYYIB, *while whispering something to him. He nods in assent.*

PRESENTER (*on screen and on stage, pretending to surprise* ABU AL-TAYYIB *with a spontaneous interview*). What a coincidence! We are honoured to have the president of the Party's local branch, Abu al-Tayyib. He is here to witness the goat-distribution ceremony. Well, fairy godfather! You have overseen this generous gesture. How are the martyrs' families responding?

ABU AL-TAYYIB (*on screen and on stage*). Oh... What a surprise! Well, first of all, we must thank the media for standing with us through good times and bad. As you can see, people are happy. They're grateful. And they're optimistic that this vicious attack on us will soon come to an end. And that we'll be safe again. Our martyrs are instilled with values – the values of conviction, faith, morality and patriotism. That's why they are on the front line.

PRESENTER. Can you tell us a bit more about the scheme?

ABU AL-TAYYIB. Absolutely. It allows us to distribute a mountain goat to every family of a martyr in the local area. This provides a model for economic, social, national and human development. In future, we hope to expand the scheme, God willing. We want to extend it to families of the kidnapped and missing. Livestock supplies permitting.

PRESENTER (*on screen and on stage*). Viewers are asking –
will the scheme be extended to other regions of our beloved
homeland?

ABU AL-TAYYIB (*on screen and on stage*). We hope so.
Our vision is for every house in the nation to have its
own goat.

PRESENTER (*on screen and on stage*). Well, thank you for this
exclusive interview. Now, we'll let you get back to the
crowd. They are waiting anxiously to hear your speech.

VILLAGERS (*in unison*). With our souls, with our blood, we
sacrifice ourselves for you, our leader! We sacrifice ourselves
for you, our country!

ABU AL-TAYYIB (*on screen and on stage*). Good afternoon,
comrades. First and last, the nation! Above all else, the
nation!

Applause.

Today we are brought together by more than martyrdom.
We are here to celebrate. We have died with honour. We have
sacrificed ourselves, and we reap the rewards of the martyr.
Noble comrades, every day our village offers up new martyrs
– as if we are the only village fighting. And we shall fight.
We shall fight to the last child, the last woman, the last
grandfather. You know the great organisation, Martyrs
Without Borders. It has nominated the village for an award –
for giving the most martyrs in a single day. With luck, we
might win the title. And if we do, what an honour!

There is the sound of recorded ululations, and the WOMEN
jump in surprise.

Now, we are here today to pay tribute. To offer thanks. The
martyrs have entrusted their families to us. They ask for no
material recompense, only moral support. Pillars of the nation,
let us step forward to receive the recognition we deserve.

ABU AL-TAYYIB *gestures to a* BODYGUARD, *holds the
list of names, to begin the distribution. As each name is read
out, another* BODYGUARD *presents a goat.*

BODYGUARD. Abu Ahmad… Imm Aziz… Abu Rami… Abu Ala'… Imm Ghassan…

ZAHRA *steps forward to take receipt of the goat.*

Abu Muhammad… Abu Muhammad…?

ABU MUHAMMAD 2. We're both called Abu Muhammad. That one might be mine…

BODYGUARD. It doesn't make any difference.

ABU MUHAMMAD 2. Up to you.

ABU MUHAMMAD 2 *takes the allotted goat. He looks doubtfully towards the other goat that* ABU MUHAMMAD 1 *has taken.*

BODYGUARD. Imm Nabil.

ABU ALA'. Where is our acclaimed teacher now, has he nothing to say? Shame on him!

ABU AL-REEM. I bet he is at home, hiding.

ABU AHMAD. Did you get a billy or a nanny?

ABU JAMAL. Keep it down!

ABU ALA'. Abu Firas has run away.

ABU AL-REEM. Yes, because the government is 'exploiting us' and 'doesn't treat us well'.

ABU AL-TAYYIB. God forgive him.

ABU AHMAD. He ought to be here.

IMM MARWAN. It won't walk with me. Come on, sweetie. Chop, chop!

Noises of encouragement.

Come on. Look, there are your brothers and sisters. They miss you. See, they're waiting for you. Come on, sweetheart!

ABU LU'AY. Yeah, there's a goat here for the venerable schoolmaster. Although I'm sure he won't deign to come and pick it up.

ABU AL-REEM. No, not until he buries his son.

ABU RAMI. Or when he finally realises his son is dead, a martyr.

ABU MUHAMMAD 2. He should be ashamed.

ABU RAMI. Abu Ahmad's goat is the biggest out of the whole lot. That seems a bit unfair.

IMM MAZEN. How old was Ahmad?

IMM AZIZ. It's because he was tall.

IMM RAMI. Can you help me get this one home?

ABU KARIM. We all make mistakes. Abu Firas is hiding at home because he's embarrassed.

ABU AL-REEM. Who do I believe, Abu Firas or my son? My son called me on the phone. 'Dad, I've got them right here,' he says, 'I'm going to chop them to bits.' I told him, 'Good for you, son. You're a hero!'

ABU AL-TAYYIB. Boys, Imm Rami is trying to get home, please help her with her goat.

IMM SALMA. When I heard my son's voice... He said, 'Don't cry, Mum. Don't wear black. I'm coming home a martyr. God will reward you, you'll be the mother of a martyr.'

IMM JAMAL. Oh, have you heard about Imm Suhayl? You'll never guess. Her boy, Suhayl, she's been selling his clothes. She said they were brand new, he'd never worn them. Isn't that awful? Hey, your one's putting her head on my goat's bottom! Get her off!

The PRESENTER *approaches* ABU ALA', *who has just taken receipt of his goat.*

PRESENTER (*on stage and on screen*). You're one of the first of the lucky people to be chosen for this generous scheme. Can you tell us how you're feeling?

ABU ALA' (*on stage and on screen, as if giving a speech*). May our martyrs rest in peace. Our hearts grieve deeply for them. They were the victims of merciless terrorists. Our nation is only for the noble, only for the brave. And this is the proof! (*Gestures to the goat.*)

PRESENTER (*on stage and on screen*). That's wonderful. Are you happy with your goat?

ABU ALA'. Very happy. We are all ready to be martyrs. We are all willing to protect this pure soil, and our father, the Leader. We are all martyrs.

The PRESENTER *turns to* ABU RAMI.

PRESENTER (*on stage and on screen*). How are you feeling?

ABU RAMI. Hard to know what to say, to be honest. I'm proud and sad at the same time, really.

PRESENTER (*on stage and on screen*). What are you going to do with your goat? What do you think it has to offer you?

ABU RAMI. It will enrich the family financially, and add to our monthly income. And it will remind me of my son's heroism and stubbornness.

When the distribution is complete, ABU AL-TAYYIB *signals to the* PRESENTER *to stop filming.* ABU AL-TAYYIB *turns towards the* VILLAGERS. *He has difficulty getting their attention thanks to the presence of the goats.*

ABU AL-TAYYIB (*on stage*). I hope everyone has received their token of appreciation. Before we all head home, please gather for a moment. Let us open our hearts, and watch this interview. (*To* MUDAR.) Mudar, son, turn it on.

The screen shows a pre-recorded interview with ABU FIRAS. *He looks broken, and appears to be reading from a piece of paper in front of him. The* VILLAGERS *are astonished.*

ABU FIRAS (*on screen*). 'My name is Ibrahim. I wish to apologise for my behaviour on the day of my son's burial. My son, the martyr. What I said that day was an insult – an insult to my son's memory, to my village, and to martyrdom. I wish to confirm that I have no relationship whatsoever with any group or party that denigrates your sons, or their sacrifices. I hope you will accept this apology. Nothing can shake my faith in our government, in our army, and in our principles, in times of war and peace.'

VOICE OF PRESENTER. And are you going to bury your son?

ABU FIRAS (*on screen*). My martyred son Firas will be buried, and I formally take back any previous demands I made.

VOICE OF PRESENTER. Do you regret... (what you did)?

The end of the recording is covered up by whistles and the bleating of goats.

Scene Eight – Blood

Night. Inside IMM GHASSAN*'s house. The electricity is off. Candlelight. The house is humbly furnished. Photos of* ABU GHASSAN *and Ghassan hang on the walls, a black ribbon over the corner of each frame, and a blown-up photo of* ZAHRA *and* ADNAN*'s wedding, with* ZAHRA*'s wedding dress made of military drill.*

IMM GHASSAN *has a large tray in her lap and is mechanically sorting rice.* ZAHRA *enters and turns on the television, showing an interview about 'the conspiracy against the nation'. She sits down in an armchair and takes up her knitting, made of the coarse black yarn she was making in Scene Two.* IMM GHASSAN *puts down the tray, goes over to the television and turns it off. She leaves the room, then comes back and resumes what she was doing.* ZAHRA *looks annoyed, sighs, and continues knitting.*

The goat is present. Whenever it tries to climb onto any of the furniture, ZAHRA *gently pulls it down. Some time goes by.*

ZAHRA (*without looking at* IMM GHASSAN). It puts me on edge, having the TV off, and that's not good for the baby. Aren't you worried about the baby? (*Pause.*) If it's a boy, I'll

call him Ghassan. If it's a girl, Bushra, after my sister. I hope
it's a girl. Every time I think of her I pray that God will
punish them. She'd never even killed a chicken. And the
monsters killed her, because she was a state employee. They
drink the same water, learn from the same schoolbooks, then
they kill us. They're no opposition, they are criminals and
traitors. (*Pause*.)

If I had finished my studies, I'd have got a government job
and I would probably have been killed too. Maybe I wouldn't
have married Adnan, I wouldn't be pregnant, and we wouldn't
be here now. God will punish them. (*Pause*.) My mum wants
to come and see the goat tomorrow, on her way back from the
shrine in our village. Would you believe it, they've heard
about this thing with Abu Firas? She's wondering if she should
take a vow of silence too, for my sister. But she's like me, she
can't stand silence. She told me she made a vow to slaughter
a chicken for me because I got a job. I can't stand the sight of
blood though, it makes me want to throw up. The sight of
slaughter really scares me. They say the terrorists want to kill
us, one by one, based on what's on our ID card, then play
football with our heads. (*Pause*.) I hope it's a boy… But
women are fighting as well now. If I wasn't pregnant, I'd go
and fight too, don't you think? (*Pause*.) Oh, I wish you could
talk to me a bit, I'm fed up! I don't miss you nagging me all
the time, obviously. But you can't stop us watching TV. When
the baby arrives it'll be different, that's what's keeping me
going. I'm just dying to see him.

Pause. ZAHRA *gets up to move television cables out of the
way of the voracious goat.*

Imm Aziz's ate the phone cable. She is worried her youngest
son will call, and she won't be able to answer. She can't look
after herself, let alone take care of a goat. It's like you have
to plan your whole life to suit the goat.

The goat makes for the television. ZAHRA *struggles to coax
it away.* IMM GHASSAN *watches them.*

See, even she wants to watch TV. God, she is strong. Aren't
you scared of her? (*Laughs at the thought that occurred to her.*)

Hey, if she jumped on you, then would you say something?
Maybe you can talk to her. Seeing as it's because of Ghassan
that we've got her. (*Goes back to her knitting*.) Tell you the
truth, I'm not that keen on babies. I feel like I'm about to lay
an egg. But I want to become a mother like the rest of you.
You are respected. It can be a hero, like the martyrs. There are
better days ahead. Otherwise they wouldn't have given me a
job as teacher. Aren't you happy for me? Or are you upset
about Abu Firas? I just don't get you. The government won't
let a silly thing like this get out of hand. People were reassured
by the video. If he wasn't an old friend of the family, I'd tell
the security services what he said last time he was here.
(*Pause*.) If you're going to stay silent, I'm going to keep
talking. What exactly was the vow you made? We heard about
Ghassan. You went into your room, and you didn't come out
until Adnan called. You said, 'God avenge your brother's
death.' That you'd never forgive them. Something like –
'There's nothing else worth saying.' And Adnan promised to
avenge him. The neighbours started coming around, but you
hardly made a noise. Next time Adnan called, I told him, 'Your
mum's refusing to speak.' Isn't that how –

ZAHRA *notices what* IMM GHASSAN *is doing*.

Hey! You're throwing out the good rice and keeping the bad.
(*Hurries to collect up the rice*.) People are dying of hunger!
(*Puts the good rice back onto the tray*.) Now you'll have to
separate it all over again. (*Goes back to her knitting*.) If we
all decided to stop talking, like you, the whole country would
be mute. (*Pause*.) Oh go on, for Adnan's sake, let's switch on
the TV. *Interview of the Week* will be on, then *Red Line*.

IMM GHASSAN *doesn't reply*.

Once I've given birth, I'm going to watch TV all day. I hear
the news whenever I close my eyes anyway. It's all here, in
my head. I can even picture what's going on in the war. I can
picture Adnan… I can see him fighting. I can see the boys,
crawling through the mud to get to the terrorists' hideout.
I even get this music playing in my head when they're
moving – boom-tararam, boom-tararam. Honestly, I could do

the whole news broadcast myself. Mum reckons I should
have been a presenter. 'When that presenter gets shot,
reporting from the front lines, you should apply for her job.'
I'll have to ask Abu al-Tayyib where I'd be most useful to
the Party. You can't ignore Abu al-Tayyib when he wants to
talk to you, you know. You could at least hear him out.
(*Pause*.)

If only this goat could talk. Pss, pss! Hey, you! Can you
understand me? Maybe we shouldn't make her stay on the
ground. Maybe she could sit on the sofa.

IMM GHASSAN *observes the goat.*

Maybe we're not looking after her properly. Imm Nader has
made a cage for hers. Have you ever had a goat before? Do
you know how to milk it? That turns my stomach.
Pregnancy. Come on, let's watch some TV, find something
that'll entertain her at least. (*Thinks*.) Where do they, you
know…? (*Thinks*.) You should try and take her out, if you
can manage it. I don't have time. What do they eat, anyway?

ZAHRA *puts down her knitting, gets up, goes into the
kitchen, and returns with a plate of lettuce. She places it in
front of the goat, nervous of getting too close. The goat eats.*

Just smell her, though. Maybe we should give her a bath.
Could you do it? You know, I found her in Ghassan's room
today? It's a miracle, she knew straight away. (*Jumps up and
grabs the newspaper from the goat, then opens it*.) Hey! Aw,
she was eating the crossword. She's bored, poor thing.
(*Regards the goat*.) Honestly now, do you find her pretty? Do
you think the baby will end up with a goat-shaped
birthmark? (*Pause*.) How are we going to sleep, with all the
noise she makes?

ZAHRA *returns to sewing together her knitted pieces,
picking it up to examine her progress.*

My mum didn't like it. She said it would be nicer if I made
it out of material. I collected lots of scraps from the
martyrs' uniforms, but there's more boots coming back than

anything else. (*Thinks*.) I'm not going to wash it. (*Pause*.) I should make one for the goat, and one for the baby. Why didn't I think of that? See, if you were talking, you'd have told me.

IMM GHASSAN *calmly tips the rice onto the floor, infuriating* ZAHRA. IMM GHASSAN *places her head on her hand, closing her eyes as if she does not want to listen to* ZAHRA *any more. The electricity cuts out.* ZAHRA, *annoyed, lights a candle.* ZAHRA *is sewing, and pricks her finger on the needle. It draws blood.* ZAHRA *watches as blood gushes abundantly.* ZAHRA *screams.* IMM GHASSAN *does not hear her. The blood drips onto the floor, but* IMM GHASSAN *does not see it. In fright,* ZAHRA *drops her knitting. She cannot believe it, and jumps up in terror.* IMM GHASSAN *does not look at her.* ZAHRA *runs outside.*

The landline rings. IMM GHASSAN *opens her eyes.* ZAHRA *returns with a wet face, dripping water. She answers the phone.*

(*On the telephone*.) Hello? Hello, love. How are you? No, first tell me how you are… When are you coming to see us…? What's wrong?

ZAHRA *hands the receiver to* IMM GHASSAN.

It's Adnan. He wants to speak to you urgently. Talk to him! It's your son, for goodness' sake.

IMM GHASSAN *hesitates, then puts the phone to her ear.*

VOICE OF ADNAN. Mum, listen. Good news. This is for Ghassan! We didn't let them have his blood for free.

A young man can be heard begging ADNAN *for mercy. The sound of a gunshot.*

IMM GHASSAN *puts down the phone on the candle, and it goes out.*

Scene Nine – Morgue

*Hospital morgue. Darkness. The creak of a large door opening.
Enter* ABU KARIM *and* ABU FIRAS. *They are not visible in
the darkness.* ABU KARIM *opens the drawer that contains
Firas's body.* ABU KARIM *leaves. The door creaks closed
behind him. Just as the door closes, a faint neon light comes on,
showing* ABU FIRAS *in front of Firas's body, the face covered.
The floor of the morgue is covered in closed coffins, or bodies
wrapped in shrouds and laid on the floor.* ABU FIRAS *silently
touches the body through the fabric; he can't make out any of
the limbs. He moans in fear and grief. He pulls back the shroud
to reveal rocks and severed limbs. He stares in horror. He
re-covers the body. He tries to whisper a few words to him, but
they come out unclear. He raises his head. His eyes are filled
with tears.*

ABU FIRAS. Firas… It's you. They tried to stop me seeing
you. What happened to you? Where have you gone? It is too
much to bear. Can you hear me? (*Raises the shroud a little,
then immediately puts it back.*) Where is the rest of my son?
These rocks are covered in your blood… Those dogs, they
did this to you. I fought the world to see you. How come
I never knew you, and now I want to know you? Talk to me.
Tell me what happened. Who took you away? (*Pause.*) This
isn't… Nothing… Dogs… My son, left to be eaten by dogs.
(*Thinks, as if something has occurred to him.*) 'Leave them
for the dogs,' I told him. But it was you, you were left for the
dogs. Answer me! I had to say goodbye, I can't let you go
without seeing your face. And please, Firas. Don't be angry
at me. Forgive me. May God be with you.

Silence. ABU FIRAS *murmurs his prayers, with his hands
on Firas's body. He makes his way to the door. The door is
closed from the outside. He tries to open it, but it is closed.
He bangs several times, but no one opens.*

(*Whispering.*) Abu Karim… Abu Karim.

ABU FIRAS *bangs again, harder this time. He tries to shove
open the door, but it does not budge. He screams.*

Abu Karim! Open the door. I am inside. Someone open the door. Abu Karim!

VOICE OF ABU KARIM. Did you pay entry and exit?

ABU FIRAS (*angrily*). Open the door!

VOICE OF ABU KARIM. Don't you want to stay with your son? Don't you want to find out what happened?

ABU FIRAS (*angrily*). I need to come out so I can find out! Open the door!

VOICE OF ABU KARIM. I am not getting up for free.

ABU FIRAS. Crooks, cheats! Open this door.

VOICE OF ABU KARIM. It is open. You are just not strong enough.

ABU FIRAS. You and your boss, you planned this together!

VOICE OF ABU KARIM. You are only here because he took pity on you. He didn't have to let you in. Go on, push it. Push! There's no other way out.

ABU FIRAS *attempts to push open the door.*

You're a coward! You couldn't spend half an hour in there before you started crying. You don't know anything. And you'll never find out. You'll have to bury him.

ABU KARIM *opens the door from the outside and* ABU FIRAS *scrambles to get out. Outside,* ABU KARIM *can be heard laughing.*

Scene Ten – Cemetery

The cemetery. Dawn. The call to prayer can be heard. The graves have flowers on them, some wilted, some fresh. Each one bears a cardboard sign showing the name of the martyr, sometimes with a photo.

ABU FIRAS *sits before Firas's grave, exhausted, staring into the earth. The grave is fresh.*

The PRESENTER *enters, wearing black clothes and sunglasses. She sits down at a grave near* ABU FIRAS, *finishes her prayers, pours water from a bottle onto the grave, then sits waiting.* ABU FIRAS *doesn't turn to her.*

PRESENTER. You kept your promise then.

> ABU FIRAS *scrutinises her, trying to remember who she is, then replies wearily.*

ABU FIRAS. I thought you were Zahra. You look different.

PRESENTER. This is what I look like.

ABU FIRAS. Your hair is black. (*Removes her sunglasses.*) And your eyes are black.

PRESENTER. No make-up, no heels. It's the anniversary of my father's death.

ABU FIRAS. God rest his soul. Was it '67 or '73? [3]

PRESENTER. It was '82, after Hama. And my two brothers. Both in Lebanon. [4] (*Pause.*) Those were real wars, Abu Firas. Back then, at least we were fighting together.

ABU FIRAS. Either way, our children are still dying.

Pause.

PRESENTER. It reminds me of a classroom. These graves, like empty seats. I am glad he was buried. After all he'd suffered. Did you sign the apology?

ABU FIRAS. You should know. You filmed the interview.

---

3. 1967: Israel's war on Egypt, Syria and Jordan. 1973: October War, launched by Egypt and Syria against Israel.

4. 1982: Massacre of Hama; 1975–90, Lebanese civil war.

PRESENTER. They only broadcast a fraction of what we filmed. So you'd better watch what you do from now on.

ABU FIRAS. Is that a threat?

PRESENTER. Everything happens for a reason.

ABU FIRAS. You didn't answer me.

PRESENTER. Is that his grave there?

ABU FIRAS. Are all the interviews you do like that?

PRESENTER. At least it's all resolved. You know, we might have footage of Firas at the front. You could ask, then you'd know for sure.

ABU FIRAS. Where could I get hold of it?

The PRESENTER *doesn't reply.*

Why would you do that, upset a father who has just buried his son? Don't you understand?

PRESENTER (*smiling reproachfully, as she makes her way towards Firas's grave*). Do you think I'm a dumb blonde? If I'm not answering, it's because I don't like what I'm hearing, not because I don't understand. Excuse me, my driver is here.

The PRESENTER *says her prayers at Firas's grave. She empties her bottle of water onto the grave, and leaves.* ABU FIRAS*'s feet sink deeper into the mud.*

The MEN *of the village enter, looking mournful, each one with his goat on a rope. One of them has painted his goat in pale military colours, another has dressed his in a soldier's khaki jacket. Another has drawn the flag on his goat. Another has stuck a flagon to the forehead of his goat. Some have decorated their goats with other accessories. Others have stuck photos of their sons onto their goats. A few bring goats as they are. The goats eat the flowers and plants on the graves.* ABU FIRAS *watches helplessly.* MEN *file in, whisper, and look suspiciously at* ABU FIRAS.

ABU LU'AY. So, the black sheep returns to the fold. Welcome back.

ABU JAMAL. Stay away. Don't talk to him.

ABU SALMA. He's just buried his son. God rest his soul.

ABU AL-REEM. He was forced to bury him.

ABU ALA'. Kept it quiet though. Instead of being proud of his son.

ABU RAMI. Another one who's stopped talking.

ABU LU'AY. After making such a fool of himself, there's nothing left to say.

ABU AL-REEM. Why isn't he talking at all?

ABU ALA'. What is there to say? We've seen him high and we've seen him low.

ABU LU'AY (*sneering*). You look good on camera. You should be an actor.

ABU AL-REEM. We all mistakes, we all have to grovel, it's fine.

ABU ALA'. I don't make mistakes.

ABU MUHAMMAD 2 (*whispering*). Yeah, he just does the grovelling.

ABU SALMA. Keep it down. We're in a cemetery. On a Friday. Have some respect.

ABU FIRAS. You know they forced me to do it. It was the only way I'd see my son.

ABU JAMAL. Who forced you?

ABU MUHAMMAD 2. Did you see him?

All look towards ABU KARIM.

ABU LU'AY (*to* ABU KARIM). What happened?

ABU KARIM. Nothing to do with me.

ABU AHMAD (*to* ABU FIRAS). You expect us to believe you now.

ABU MUHAMMAD 1. I'll never believe anything he says.

ABU JAMAL. Come on, leave it. This isn't getting us anywhere.

ABU RAMI. I'm sure Abu al-Tayyib had orders from above.

ABU AL-REEM. You wait, in a few days he'll back on TV, crying and grovelling.

ABU SALMA. What did you see?

ABU FIRAS *remains silent*.

ABU MUHAMMAD 1. We all get old, God help us. Leave him alone, he's lost it.

ABU AHMAD. Say it wasn't your son. Wouldn't you still pray for him?

ABU JAMAL. One guy went to get his son from the morgue, found a boy who was still alive. Ended up taking him home. What does it matter? He saved a boy.

ABU LU'AY. Let's go, before he does his Jehovah's Witness act. We're here to pay our respects, not to be lectured.

Some of them snigger.

ABU FIRAS. What is there to laugh about?

ABU KARIM. Have some dignity. Go home.

ABU FIRAS. Where's your dignity? You're happy to replace your son with a goat.

ABU AL-REEM. You'll get one too.

ABU AHMAD. He's jealous.

ABU MUHAMMAD 1. It's generous of them to give poor people a goat.

ABU JAMAL. It's a blessing, you don't even have to buy milk.

ABU RAMI. I don't get why they had to link the goats-thing to our sons, though. Why not just give us goats as a gift?

ABU MUHAMMAD 2. Either way, you wouldn't turn it down.

ABU MUHAMMAD 1. It's a practical gift. Like money in the bank. Or gold.

ABU MUHAMMAD 2. Better than gold.

ABU AHMAD. I don't like it either. But I'm no better than anyone else. Why not take it?

ABU JAMAL. I'd have preferred a cow.

ABU MUHAMMAD 2. I'd be too scared to turn it down.

ABU FIRAS. Thank God our sons don't know they're only worth a goat.

ABU ALA' *lunges at* ABU FIRAS. *The others surround him and pull him away.*

ABU KARIM. We should speak to Abu al-Tayyib.

ABU SALMA. Not now, when he's just had the news about al-Tayyib.

ABU FIRAS. Al-Tayyib is dead?

ABU AL-REEM. Yeah – did you think you were the only one?

ABU AHMAD. He only called him a few days ago to tell him he'd caught some terrorists, poor thing.

ABU KARIM. You're right. Best not to bother him.

ABU FIRAS *remains silent and does not move.* ABU ALA' *moves away.*

Right, the show is over. Abu Firas, time to go.

The MEN *disperse, leaving* ABU FIRAS. *He stands as if to leave, but looks hesitant as he watches the* MEN *and their goats. The* MEN *are reading the* fatiha *at their sons' graves. They clear away wilted flowers, lay new ones, and water the graves. Pause.*

(*To* ABU FIRAS.) What are you looking at?

ABU FIRAS. At you. At me. At our children. I am the one who failed to look after my son. It was me who left him to the dogs.

ABU JAMAL. God rest his soul. Don't go thinking like that.

ABU FIRAS. No, I saw him. There was nothing left of him.

ABU RAMI. Be thankful you are blessed with a martyr.

ABU AL-REEM. Don't let him fool you. He'll get you talking against the government. You wait, he'll be at it again. 'My son was scared when he called. Our sons are frightened.' Underneath, that man is a snake.

ABU FIRAS. Abu al-Reem, I am not answering that. But tonight, lay your head on your pillow, try to tell yourself that I am a liar. Deep down, you know it is all true. Don't you? Abu al-Reem? Abu Jamal? Abu Ala'?

ABU JAMAL. So what if they do get scared and phone home sometimes! This is a war, for goodness' sake!

ABU AL-REEM. It's not our problem if you don't know how to raise your children!

ABU FIRAS. I raised all of your children!

They are taken aback at this. Pause.

ABU JAMAL. So what do you want now?

ABU MUHAMMAD 2. He wants to blame the officers, he's trying to claim they left his son alone or something like that. (*Imitating* ABU FIRAS.) 'Why do you find it normal that our kids are calling and saying, we've captured terrorists… We don't know what to do… Where are the officers? Why are our children alone? It's not just one of them that this has happened to, it's all of them! Why don't they know what to do? What's happening out there? Where are we sending our boys? Why are they all calling and saying the same thing?' Isn't that right, Abu Firas?

Silence. They are taken aback at ABU MUHAMMAD 2*'s words.*

ABU JAMAL. You do a pretty good impression!

ABU AHMAD (*pulling himself together to intervene*). They're calling because our army is an ethical army. It doesn't decide to kill people just like that –

ABU MUHAMMAD 1. If that's true, Abu Ahmad, then why don't they call us every day asking what they should do? It's not that. They just call us to give us the good news.

ABU FIRAS. How come half the time they're calling when they're terrified and the other half they're sending photos showing what monsters they are! And why, when they ask us what they should do, do we never hear from them again? Why do they come back dead? Don't tell me I'm making this up! They're being left to die, I'm sure.

Silence again.

ABU JAMAL. I have nothing else to say to you except get out of our way. What a way to spend a morning!

ABU FIRAS. Can't you tell there's something going on that we're not hearing about? Don't you want to find out what it is?

The MEN *leave, muttering to themselves under their breaths.*

ABU FIRAS *is left alone, looking pensive.*

Pause.

Enter FADI, JUDE, SAMI *and* MUDAR, *carrying an enormous flag that completely blocks out everything behind it. They are talking quietly.*

SAMI. It's the longest flag in the world, we made it for the march.

MUDAR. They are going to take pictures of it from space.

ABU FIRAS *attempts to pass behind the flag and leave.*

SAMI. Sir, don't you want to be in the picture?

They quickly leave.

The flag covers the whole stage, and is then pulled away. Emptiness.

Scene Eleven – Run away

In front of IMM GHASSAN*'s house. Morning.* IMM
GHASSAN *and* IMM NABIL *are seated. The goats are tied up
by the door.* IMM GHASSAN *never takes her eyes off the goat.
Silence. The goats bleat.*

IMM NABIL. I'm always hearing things falling over, then I go
and look, and it's another thing broken. (*Pause.*) She's ruined
the settee we had by the front door. (*Pause.*) They told me she
was black. Yesterday when I went to go and milk her, I
couldn't find her – I was beside myself. Then the boys told me
she was up on the roof. How she got up there I don't know,
God help us. (*Pause.*) She follows me around, too. Wherever
I go, I find myself saying, 'This is where Abu Nabil used to
watch TV… Nabil used to sit here when he was on the
phone… Yazan used to sit here to do his homework…' They
took his clothes. God knows what for – is there anyone poorer
than us? (*Pause.*) When there's water, I fill the basin, throw it
all over myself and cry. Where else can I cry but the
bathroom? (*Pause.*) I know Yazan killed himself. And I know
everyone knows. I know they're just pretending they don't.
We're all scared. His granddad wanted to send him to the
national defence as soon as he'd done his exams, and he didn't
want to go. Imm Nader's son – you know, he's an officer – had
it in for him. I'm sure the boy was ready to explode. It was
them that killed him. We're not worth shit to them. See, they
gave us a goat to shut us up. If you open your mouth to say
anything about it, they take your next one. (*Pause.*) Morning
and night, I tell myself they've been good to us. Without them,
God knows where we'd be. Penniless and living in the
mountains, like we are now. God keep us safe in their grip,
even when it hurts. I know what you're going to say.

VILLAGE WOMEN *start to arrive at* IMM GHASSAN*'s
house.* IMM GHASSAN *gets up.* IMM NABIL *realises they
have arrived.* IMM GHASSAN *heads for the door to go
inside.*

I'll see you tomorrow.

IMM GHASSAN *goes inside.*

ZAHRA. Doesn't she want to join us?

IMM NABIL. She doesn't know how to ride a bike.

They laugh. VILLAGE WOMEN *arrive, some with their goats, continuing conversations.* ZAHRA *tidies up. They sit. The goats bleat loudly. They are decorated with accessories.*

Bye, girls.

IMM RAMI. Who's going to teach us?

IMM NABIL *leaves, feeling her way as she walks.*

IMM MARWAN. Zahra is going to get a teacher for us.

ZAHRA. That's what the village next to ours did.

IMM AZIZ. Aren't we a bit old for this?

ZAHRA. Don't be so old-fashioned.

IMM NADER. Look out, it's eating your papers.

ZAHRA *leaps up to retrieve her papers from the goat's mouth.*

ZAHRA. She'd have choked.

IMM MAZEN. They'll eat anything.

IMM RAMI. Is yours eating everything in the house too?

IMM MAZEN. I don't let mine in the house. It can eat whatever it wants outside.

IMM SALMA. Mine ate Randa's degree certificate.

IMM RAMI. They're like hoovers.

IMM MAZEN. They're not meant to go inside the house. They're dirty.

IMM RAMI. Shh, don't be rude.

IMM MAZEN. I don't care. Each one of you is dafter than the next. They're livestock, you keep them outside. You're meant to make use of them, not wait on them hand and foot. This silly twit's gone and made a bed for hers.

ZAHRA. We disagreed about this last time, and we're not going to waste time on it this meeting too.

IMM ALA'. But it's more important than the bikes.

ZAHRA. Who knows how to ride a bike?

IMM MAZEN. Imm al-Tayyib does, but he won't let her.

IMM NADER. Have you heard the news?

ZAHRA. What news?

IMM NADER. Oh, never mind then, I'd best not say.

IMM AZIZ. You're not meant to give it sugar.

IMM RAMI. She likes it. They like molasses too.

IMM AZIZ. You're not supposed to…

IMM NADER. Oh, leave her alone. Her husband won't let her feed it anything at all at home.

IMM ALA'. He's mad. He wanted to kill it a few days ago. I caught him loading his rifle. Said he couldn't sleep.

IMM MARWAN. People are saying Abu Samer killed his goat.

WOMEN. No! Can you believe it? Goodness! Was it pregnant?

IMM NADER. A lot of them have twins.

IMM AZIZ. Good lord, don't rumours spread fast in this village. That's not true.

IMM MAZEN (*whispering to* IMM NADER). I know what happened. Abu al-Tayyib has sent Kinan abroad, hasn't he?

IMM NADER *nods*.

After the news about al-Tayyib.

IMM NADER. He's not saying when the burial is…

IMM MARWAN. I heard Abu Ramez sold his.

IMM ALA'. So, it wasn't stolen, like he said?

IMM MAZEN. Who'd want to steal it?

IMM MARWAN. But they gave him such a hard time, he went to the market and bought another one that looked like it… Paid an arm and a leg for it.

IMM ALA'. What, the same one?

IMM MARWAN. No, a new one. I had my eye on theirs, it was a beauty. I can tell this isn't the same one.

ZAHRA. Right, let's get back to the cycling event.

IMM JAMAL. What's cycling got to do with peace?

ZAHRA. That's just what the event is called. All the developed countries do it.

IMM NADER. This way, they'll see that we're civilised.

IMM JAMAL. Great.

ZAHRA. We're going to be filmed for TV.

IMM ALA'. My husband won't let me.

ZAHRA. Well, he can't stop you, not this of all things… Abu al-Tayyib will have a chat with him.

IMM SALMA. What am I going to do with the goat, on the day?

IMM MAZEN. Get it a bike of its own and it can ride with us!

They laugh.

ZAHRA. Right, what did we manage to get in donations, Imm Marwan?

IMM NADER. Zahra, your goat's looking awful skinny, poor thing.

IMM JAMAL. You can't talk! Keeping yours tied up in the basement, where it never sees the light of day.

IMM NADER. The kids like to ride it.

IMM JAMAL. But you can't keep her in there, the poor thing will get rickets and go mad.

IMM NADER. My husband lets her out in the mornings. He is worried the dogs will get her.

ZAHRA. How many bikes are there in the village? Someone was meant to count them, weren't they?

IMM MARWAN. Yes. There are around twelve. The milkman has one, should I count that?

IMM MAZEN. Who buys milk any more? He'll probably have to sell the thing.

IMM ALA'. Imm Suhayl's son – he is in Sweden, he's applying for family reunification. Do you think they'll leave the goat?

IMM MAZEN. Oh, for goodness' sake.

ZAHRA. Ladies! Can we stick to the topic? We need to decide which of the tarmac roads we're going to use.

IMM RAMI (*passing her phone to* IMM AZIZ). Here, look.

IMM AZIZ. Lovely.

ZAHRA. What is it?

IMM RAMI *passes the phone to* ZAHRA.

No, we can't. The profile picture for the page this week is going to be the Mothers of Martyrs Association, not –

IMM JAMAL. Let's tease the other women a bit.

IMM RAMI. Come on, don't be annoyed. We can put up a different goat every week.

IMM MAZEN. Oh, come off it. Pictures of goats! Have you all gone mad? Honestly, you're driving me up the wall. Next thing, you'll be recording the noises they make and turning them into ringtones.

IMM ALA'. She's right, let's not get carried away.

IMM NADER. Seriously now, their droppings are ever so good for the soil.

ABU FIRAS *arrives*.

The WOMEN, *especially* ZAHRA, *are indignant*.

ABU FIRAS. Is Imm Ghassan here?

ZAHRA. We heard about your son.

IMM MARWAN. And we saw the video...

> *The* WOMEN *tell each other not to speak to* ABU FIRAS.

ABU FIRAS. Where's Imm Ghassan?

ZAHRA. I'm here. Can I help you?

ABU FIRAS (*calling out*). Imm Ghassan, are you there?

> ABU FIRAS *strides forward to call out to* IMM GHASSAN, *and the frightened* WOMEN *hastily scatter and leave.*

ZAHRA. She doesn't want to see you. See how everyone runs away from you!

ABU FIRAS (*calling out*). Imm Ghassan! Come out and talk to me!

ZAHRA. You are not coming any closer.

ABU FIRAS. I'm not talking to you. It's none of your business.

ZAHRA. Yes, it is my business. You are hurting my family. I have a baby on the way, and I want to bring it up properly. No mother would –

ABU FIRAS (*interrupting*). Imm Ghassan, come out! I know you're there.

ZAHRA. Leave my family alone, or I'll call the police.

ABU FIRAS (*to* IMM GHASSAN). When Adnan called, what did he say?

ZAHRA. Adnan avenged his brother, made us all proud. I heard the gunshot. Or are you going to tell me he was scared.

ABU FIRAS (*talking past* ZAHRA). What about Ghassan? Was his call the same? Talk to me! They're using our sons as bait.

> *Pause.* IMM GHASSAN *emerges from the door.*

ZAHRA (*to* IMM GHASSAN). You don't believe this rubbish.

ABU FIRAS. The officers are leaving our sons to die. Probably without weapons. They are sacrificing them.

ZAHRA. Shame! You were filmed, apologising. (*To* IMM GHASSAN.) Tell him to go away! I don't want to –

ABU FIRAS. I was forced into it. The boys need help.

ZAHRA. Who are you to decide? Listen to what we want.

The landline rings. ZAHRA *goes inside to answer it.* ABU FIRAS *moves closer to* IMM GHASSAN *who backs away, flustered.*

ABU FIRAS. What did Adnan say last time he rang?

ZAHRA (*off, on phone*). Hello? How are you? Darling, is everything okay?

IMM GHASSAN *and* ABU FIRAS *pay attention when they realise it is* ADNAN *calling.*

Your mum won't say a word. Abu Firas is driving us up the wall, he ought to be… (*Beat.*) Okay, okay. Imm Ghassan, Imm Ghassan!

ZAHRA *returns angrily and holds out the phone.* IMM GHASSAN *hesitates, then takes it and places it to her ear.* IMM GHASSAN *scowls, not knowing what to say.*

(*Speaking past* IMM GHASSAN, *into receiver.*) Even if you die, she won't speak.

ABU FIRAS. What's happening to the boys? Ask him.

ZAHRA *brings her head closer to the receiver so she can also hear.*

ZAHRA. Talk to her, she can hear you. (*Ululates.*) Congratulations, you're a hero! How many?

ABU FIRAS. What's going on?

IMM GHASSAN*'s face darkens as she is listening.*

ZAHRA (*to* ADNAN). Kill them! We –

ADNAN *tells her off, and* ZAHRA *stops. She waits for* IMM GHASSAN, *who stays silent.*

(*To* IMM GHASSAN.) He's caught some terrorists. He's asking you what to do. Speak! Go on. Why won't you answer him? (*To* ADNAN.) Don't kill them straight away. Get them to talk, and then... And send us a picture, of you with them –

ABU FIRAS. Run! Run! Tell him to run! Is he surrounded? He'll be killed. (*Raises his voice so that* ADNAN *can hear him.*) Run! They don't care about you. Just get out! (*Confused.*) Son, get out! Firas, get out! Run! Run!

ABU FIRAS *sits down, devastated.* ZAHRA *doesn't understand what is happening.*

IMM GHASSAN (*speaking, at last*). Run!

ZAHRA (*to* IMM GHASSAN). What? You're mad. (*To* ADNAN.) If you don't kill them, I'll kill myself.

IMM GHASSAN (*to* ADNAN). Don't call again. Don't tell anyone. Just get away!

IMM GHASSAN *hangs up.*

ZAHRA. You're a traitor.

ABU FIRAS (*to* IMM GHASSAN). You listened to me...

ZAHRA. I don't believe it!

ZAHRA *tries to call back, but she is unable to get through.* ABU FIRAS *and* IMM GHASSAN *exchange glances.*

You're not one of us, you are a criminal, one of them. Of course, you don't watch TV. My baby's father... a coward? Shame! I will kill it, before it's even born. Get out of here!

ZAHRA *goes inside, in a fury. The sound of things breaking can be heard.* IMM GHASSAN *hurls away the handset and it breaks.*

ABU KARIM *arrives, as if sent for.* ABU FIRAS *and* IMM GHASSAN *ignore him.* ABU KARIM *look around, puzzled.*

ABU FIRAS (*to* IMM GHASSAN). You won't regret it. You and I, we are still alive, that's our shame. (*His voice fading away as he leaves.*)

*IMM GHASSAN remains standing where she is. The
breaking sounds continue inside the house.* ABU KARIM
goes into the house.

*The goat butts its head against the wall, and the house
shakes.*

Scene Twelve – Gesture

In front of ABU FIRAS*'s house. Middle of the day. Lots of goats.
The* VILLAGERS *are gathered with* ABU AL-TAYYIB*'s*
BODYGUARDS, *one of whom is standing by* ABU FIRAS*'s
front door holding a goat on a rope. The* PRESENTER *and*
CAMERAMAN *are also present.*

ABU AL-TAYYIB *arrives and they clear a path for him.
Applause.*

ABU AL-TAYYIB *stands smiling beneficently as the*
BODYGUARD *knocks at* ABU FIRAS*'s front door. They wait.*
ABU FIRAS *doesn't open. The* BODYGUARD *knocks again.
The* CAMERAMAN *films the door as he knocks, and when it
doesn't open, turns to film the faces of the audience and their
goats. The* PRESENTER *is impatient.*

PRESENTER. Abu al-Tayyib, shall we head off? We only have
    ten minutes.

ABU AL-TAYYIB. We will not be long.

ABU JAMAL. Maybe he's not in?

IMM JAMAL. Or he is too embarrassed.

IMM MAZEN (*quietly*). You know, in some villages people are
    getting sheep.

IMM JAMAL (*quietly*). Yeah, but in some places, all they got
    was a bit of rice and bulghur.

BODYGUARD (*to* ABU AL-TAYYIB). Sir, shall we go in?

Still smiling, ABU AL-TAYYIB *gestures that there is no need for violence while the camera is present.*

IMM MARWAN (*quietly*). Some people got money to set up a little shop.

IMM MAZEN (*quietly*). Yeah, and they stocked it with goods, too.

IMM JAMAL (*quietly*). Some people deserve better than others, apparently.

ABU ALA' (*to* ABU AL-TAYYIB). Comrade, did you hear about his performance at the cemetery?

ABU AL-TAYYIB *ignores him.*

BODYGUARD. Maybe he doesn't want to open up?

ABU ALA'. After everything he's done, he doesn't deserve a goat.

ABU AHMAD. I'm just here to see the missile.

ABU AL-REEM. My brother's in the command, he said the missile takes only twenty-three minutes to reach its target.

IMM NADER (*quietly*). My sister got a clock.

IMM RAMI (*quietly*). Batteries included?

IMM AZIZ (*quietly*). Look what that presenter is wearing today.

ABU AL-TAYYIB. He must be getting ready. Abu Karim, are you sure he is at home?

ABU KARIM *nods.*

IMM MAZEN (*quietly*). My sister got two packs of tobacco. I swear! But her husband doesn't smoke. She wants to sell them – do you want them?

IMM RAMI. They get all this stuff, just because we got goats?

ABU AHMAD (*quietly*). It's still nothing, given what they've lost. Many families don't even get back the body of their martyr.

ABU ALA' (*wondering*). Do you think Abu Firas really doesn't want one?

ABU MUHAMMAD 1. They said we'd get to see him accepting his goat.

ABU MUHAMMAD 2. Same as us.

ABU AL-REEM. Why stand around waiting for him, comrade? He doesn't deserve it.

ABU AL-TAYYIB. Comrade Abu al-Reem, we are not here only for him. There's another important event today. We didn't want to bother the TV crew twice, so we are killing two birds with one stone. In any case, it is important for people to see this, because the story about him got out somehow.

ABU AL-REEM *falls silent, looking resentful. The* BODYGUARD *knocks again at* ABU FIRAS*'s door.* ABU FIRAS *yanks open the door, suddenly and roughly. He is wearing a vest and shorts. The* VILLAGERS *are embarrassed and uncomfortable at the sight.* ABU AL-TAYYIB *is surprised. The* VILLAGERS' *reactions range from mockery to trepidation.*

IMM NABIL. What on earth is going on?

Live coverage plays on the screen. The CAMERAMAN *zooms to avoid* ABU FIRAS*'s body, focusing instead on his face and on the other people present.*

On stage, BODYGUARD *beckons* IMM AZIZ, *who is carrying a bag.* IMM AZIZ, *ululating, takes out a handful of rice and throws it festively over* ABU AL-TAYYIB *and the* PRESENTER. *The* PRESENTER *steps forward and thrusts a microphone in front of* ABU AL-TAYYIB.

IMM ALA' (*looking at the rice on the ground*). I hope you sorted that properly.

ABU KARIM. Abu Firas, go and put on something decent.

ABU AL-TAYYIB. Abu Firas, you are today's lucky winner. We are here today to present you with this goat, as a token of

our gratitude. Your family has given so much to the nation.
And we want you to be with us to witness a very special
surprise. First, please say a few words for the occasion.

ABU MUHAMMAD 2 (*sarcastically*). This will be a once-in-a-
lifetime event.

ABU FIRAS *stands there without replying*.

ABU AL-TAYYIB. Abu Firas, what's up? Do you want to get
changed? We can wait.

ABU FIRAS *doesn't reply*.

ABU KARIM. Comrade, we don't have long.

ABU AL-TAYYIB. I hope we have not said anything to upset
you. We have come to see you to celebrate your return to the
fold. Everyone is so proud of what you said in the video.
We want to renew the bonds of patriotism which tie us all
together. Everyone makes mistakes. An honourable person is
one who recognises their mistakes.

ABU FIRAS *does not speak, but looks intently at those
assembled*.

ABU ALA'. I told you he wouldn't accept the goat.

ABU AL-REEM. Well, he doesn't need it.

ABU AL-TAYYIB. Your son has a right to be honoured. Do not
throw away that right. You could always sacrifice it at a
shrine. Do not set a bad example to young people. We give to
our village, and our village gives back. Don't spoil that. The
goat is our gift to you in Firas's name.

ABU KARIM. We can't waste time sweet-talking you today.

ABU AL-TAYYIB. Abu Firas, if you refuse the goat, there will
be consequences.

ABU MUHAMMAD 2. Even I know that.

ABU AL-TAYYIB. You made a promise in public, to them and
to me. I am sure you don't want to renege on it.

ABU AHMAD. You made a promise, Abu Firas? What was it?

ABU AL-REEM. When they say 'everyone gets a goat', that means... everyone gets one.

ABU ALA'. Abu Firas always has to be different. Each goat is for someone's son. This goat is for Imm Nabil's son. This one is for Abu al-Reem's son. This one is Suhayla's son. This one is Muhammad, this one is Ahmad...

ABU FIRAS. You are right, Abu al-Tayyib. We are all parents, we are all one family, and we all need to be absolved. Take my goat. Consider it a gift. In return, tell us all the truth – about the sons, the phone calls, the deaths.

ABU AL-TAYYIB. We had an agreement. You are breaking it in front of everyone.

IMM AZIZ. He is mad.

ABU FIRAS. No, the mad ones go on TV. They send their boys to their deaths, but they cry when they die. And then they shut up as soon as they get a goat.

ABU AL-REEM. I knew this would go badly.

ABU AL-TAYYIB. I am trying to give him another chance, but he is not taking it. Did you see what just happened? How we approached him, and then how he repaid our generosity? I just hope no one will blame us now if we have to take any further steps, albeit against one of our most respected figures, in order to protect our country's honour.

The VILLAGERS *mutter disapprovingly. The* BODYGUARDS *approach* ABU FIRAS *to hustle him back inside the house. Patriotic music plays.*

ABU FIRAS (*trying to talk to the* BODYGUARDS). We are the mad ones. We cheer when our sons kill the enemy. And their parents gloat when they kill our sons. Who wants my goat?

The VILLAGERS *shift awkwardly and the* BODYGUARDS *shove* ABU FIRAS *inside.* ABU FIRAS *closes the door.*

ABU AL-TAYYIB. Keep banging your head against the wall, Abu Firas. Soon, we'll come and do it for you.

ABU AL-TAYYIB *looks at his watch in agitation and makes a sign to the* PRESENTER, *who nods to the* CAMERAMAN.

On screen, a fake video is showing ABU FIRAS *accepting the goat.*

On stage, SAMI *enters at a run.*

SAMI. It's coming, it's coming!

PRESENTER (*on screen, shouting*). Right now, ladies and gentlemen, we're about to –

The PRESENTER*'s voice is drowned out by the noise.*

On screen, the CAMERAMAN *films the sky.*

On stage, the VILLAGERS *whistle and yell increasingly loudly, but the missile is louder still.* ZAHRA *arrives.* ABU AL-TAYYIB*'s voice becomes audible.*

ABU AL-TAYYIB (*on stage, shouting, but we only hear his voice from the screen*). That is the sound of a Scud missile, soaring through the sky over our village. Bang on schedule! The army is famous for its precision. As is the leadership – and as are the people. Just look at this – an awesome spectacle. We can just glimpse the Scud on its twenty-three-minute flight. We are so proud of our Scud.

PRESENTER (*on screen*). Viewers, as we speak, a Scud missile is passing over the village. The 196th battalion launched it in the presence of the regional party leader, the mayor, the municipal councillors, and villagers young and old.

On stage, IMM SALMA *kneels down and kisses the ground.*

On screen, rousing music. ABU SALMA *makes his way towards the* PRESENTER *and stands in front of the camera.*

ABU SALMA (*on screen, eyes brimming with tears of joy*). It was my son who launched it!

On stage, pandemonium. All heads are raised to the sky. The goats bleat loudly. As the missile continues past the village, the VILLAGERS *move robotically to follow it. They exit.*

The screen continues to show the missile's flight, then turns off the moment it explodes.

The stage is empty.

Outside ABU FIRAS*'s house, the goat is tied up.* ABU FIRAS *opens the door and he is surprised to find it there.* ABU FIRAS *unties the goat and leaves it to escape. He then looks up at the sky. The goat stays in front of the door.* ABU FIRAS *shoos it away, but the goat remains resolutely next to him.*

ABU FIRAS *runs inside and closes the door behind him.*

The goat stays outside his house.

Scene Thirteen – Hero

IMM GHASSAN*'s house. Night-time. The room is full of furniture and electrical appliances, much more than before.* ZAHRA *enters carrying a tray of food and puts it down. She turns off the light and leaves.* IMM GHASSAN *gets up and lights a candle.* ADNAN *enters, hair wet, and sits down to eat.* IMM GHASSAN *watches him.* ADNAN *eats in a strange manner, without stopping. Whenever he finishes what is in front of him,* ZAHRA *brings him more.*

ADNAN (*coldly*). Am I clean now?

IMM GHASSAN *is silent.*

Did you answer me? (*Pause. Shouting.*) Where is it?

ZAHRA *rushes in and hands him the blanket she knitted.* ADNAN *touches it, sniffs it and immediately casts it away.*

Get that out of here, it smells disgusting.

ZAHRA *takes it away.*

Mum, I didn't hear you.

IMM GHASSAN *does not respond*, ADNAN *pulls her forcefully towards him by the arm, which terrifies her. He kisses her hand.*

When I speak to you, answer me.

ZAHRA *enters and sits down.*

Answer me!

ZAHRA. Ever since –

ADNAN *glares at her, and she falls silent.*

ADNAN. Your turn's coming next.

IMM GHASSAN. There's nothing to say.

ADNAN. People talk.

IMM GHASSAN. You should've listened to what I wasn't saying.

ADNAN (*taking the food in his hands and eating*). Great!

IMM GHASSAN. You'll always lose when you're up against people who have nothing to lose.

ADNAN (*the food drips from his elbows*). Riddles too… I should applaud.

IMM GHASSAN. I didn't ask you to. And you didn't ask me. You decided, and you called.

ADNAN. So, I didn't kill that man for my brother? Because you'd made a vow? I killed him because of a misunderstanding.

ZAHRA (*pause*). Because you're a hero.

ADNAN (*throwing food at ZAHRA*). Look, stupid. Why didn't you catch it? You shouldn't let food fall on the floor. Heroes don't run away, do they?

ZAHRA *doesn't know what to do.*

Clear it up! A schoolteacher like you shouldn't be dirty.

ZAHRA *quickly gets up. Pause.*

(*To* IMM GHASSAN.) You still haven't answered me.

IMM GHASSAN. About what?

ADNAN. About everything. Why I'm here. Why did I kill the guy if not for you? Why is the house full of stuff? What are you two celebrating me for? Why is there a goat outside?

IMM GHASSAN. People who talk don't last long. But you're going to stay, so keep your voice down.

Pause. ZAHRA *returns.*

ZAHRA. Sweetheart, calm down, I –

ADNAN. Sit down, you! And put this in your mouth.

He hands her a large piece of food, which ZAHRA *takes.*

Is the power off?

IMM GHASSAN. Did anyone see you?

ADNAN. Only Imm Ahmad... And God.

IMM GHASSAN. Imm Ahmad won't say anything.

ADNAN (*laughing in a strange manner*). Nor will God!

IMM GHASSAN. Abu al-Tayyib sent Kinan away, and we all pretended we didn't know.

Pause.

ADNAN (*to* ZAHRA). Haven't you finished your mouthful yet? How's our little hero going to get enough to eat? Don't you want him to be a martyr too?

ZAHRA. Honestly, I'm full.

ADNAN. I know better than you.

IMM GHASSAN. It's not good for the b–

ADNAN. He was up against the wall. No – when I first came into the room he was sitting like this, eating. On the floor. His wife was in the bedroom. His daughter was younger than you... (*To* ZAHRA.) ...and prettier.

ZAHRA. Who?

IMM GHASSAN. I don't want to hear.

ADNAN. The boys came in and dragged the girl outside.
    Whatever, she got what she deserved. The dad lost his mind.

IMM GHASSAN. Stop talking!

ADNAN. His wife kissed my feet... I think it was this one first.

ZAHRA. What are you talking about?

> IMM GHASSAN *gets up to leave but* ADNAN *grabs her
> and sits her back down.*

ADNAN. When the hero's talking, you sit and listen! We're
    fighting and getting killed and liberating territory and
    storming enemy hideouts for you, so when we talk you can
    damn well sit still and pay attention. The guys dragged her
    outside too. I don't know what happened to her. The girl,
    I know, because I heard. The father... Against the wall... As
    well... He tried to kiss my feet! I said to him, 'It wasn't easy
    for my mum to lose her first son. And it isn't easy for me that
    she's decided to stop talking till we've avenged him. So,
    you'll have to wait a few moments while I call her...'

ZAHRA. Adnan, what's wrong with you?

> ADNAN *throws food at her.* ZAHRA *bursts into tears.*

IMM GHASSAN. Have you got no shame any more?

> ADNAN *laughs.*

I don't want to –

> ADNAN *suddenly leaps up, and* ZAHRA *and* IMM
> GHASSAN *recoil in fright. He goes over to the fridges
> which are in the room, opens them all until he finds the real
> one, gets out some more food and returns.*

ADNAN. Who's bringing them to the village?

> *Neither reply, so* ADNAN *kicks the fridges.*

IMM GHASSAN. Don't do that! Zahra's bought them ready to
    furnish your house when you come back.

ADNAN. Who looted them?

IMM GHASSAN. Adnan!

ADNAN. Well, this is strange. Why are you keeping things from me? Who's the piece of shit that's cornered the market around here? Do you think I don't know how and where it's all coming from?

IMM GHASSAN. We don't know.

ZAHRA. Nabil.

ADNAN. That fucking cunt. I swear to God I knew.

IMM GHASSAN. Adnan!

ADNAN (*to* IMM GHASSAN). Fuck, fuck, fucking fuck. Cunt, fucking cunt. Do you know how Nabil died? He became a martyr while he was looting... (*To* ZAHRA.) Get me some water!

ZAHRA *gets up. She leaves the room.*

Where was I? Oh yeah... His face was against the wall. I told him to turn around, and I called you. Time for listeners' requests, I told you, and today you get to hear your favourite song! Bang! After everything I've seen, everything I've been through, I can safely say that was the biggest thing I've done in my life. He just crumpled up. On the spot. (*To* ZAHRA.) Where's that water, you waste of space? (*To* IMM GHASSAN.) Do you know that was the first time I've ever killed someone? No, I mean – the first time I've known I've killed someone. Do you understand?

ZAHRA *comes in, hands him the water.*

Bless your hands!

ZAHRA *turns to go back out.* ADNAN *makes a loud noise through the water he is drinking straight from the bottle, to indicate she should come back and sit down.* ZAHRA *sits down. He finishes the whole bottle of water.*

Ah, I've missed spending the evenings together like this. Those days were so calm, but back then we didn't know it.

ZAHRA. Hopefully things will go back to being like that, darling.

ADNAN. Let's just hope we win and manage to kill half the country. Isn't that what you want, my love? Say it, I want to hear it for myself. Don't you want us to bomb them out of existence? While they're eating. Just like this. Boom! Finished your dinner. A leg here, an arm, a head here, hair over there. Boom. That's the Scud for you. The Scud we love so much. The Scud our taxes paid for. We inherit our parents' unpaid tax, did you know that?

IMM GHASSAN *makes a move to get up but* ADNAN *stops her.*

Don't go! We haven't eaten yet.

ADNAN *eats while* ZAHRA *and* IMM GHASSAN *watch him.*

How long has Abu Ghassan been dead now? Martyred, I mean – not dead.

ZAHRA. Since 1986.

ADNAN. They had an accident on the bus ride back from Hama, where he was an officer – remember why? Maybe it was to detain the people that kept coming to ask about their kids that were disappearing. You know, we're now seeing their kids at the front. We're killing them, and they're killing us. (*Sardonic.*) It's nice, Zahra – you should tell people about it at your pottery class. (*To* IMM GHASSAN.) You've worn black since the eighties. You should stop wearing black. How long since you've danced?

IMM GHASSAN. Stop all this funny business, son, please!

ZAHRA. A long time.

ADNAN *jumps up and grabs* ZAHRA*'s hand. She isn't able to resist. He starts dancing Dabkeh with her, and then grabs* IMM GHASSAN, *who refuses.*

ADNAN. It hasn't been so long for me. We shoot, we kill someone, we dance, we shoot again, dance again… Come on! Higher, higher… Faster… Come on, dance! Kill it! Down, up!

IMM GHASSAN. Stop it, the baby!

> ZAHRA *tries to extricate herself from* ADNAN, *who is pulling her along violently. He continues until she trips and falls. Terrified, she quickly sits herself up.*

ADNAN. If you can't even dance, how can you fight? (*Pause.*) Man, Nabil took that video of me killing the guy, you'd have showed that to everyone. That piece of shit Nabil used to film everything. Shame really! (*Resumes eating.*) He's got an amazing mind for business. Incredible. Films everything and sells it. You know how much he begged me to shoot him when he got injured? I couldn't do it, though. I only kill for my darling mother, don't I? Although one of our mates, really nice guy, went nuts one day and went and shot everyone in the dugout. All his friends. Then he shot himself afterwards. So, it shouldn't have been a big deal to shoot Nabil, but I still couldn't. (*Pauses and eats.*) But which idiot went and screwed everything up when we were surrounded? (*Waits for a response then raises his voice.*) Which idiot was with us? Guess! Who?

ZAHRA. I don't know.

IMM GHASSAN. Careful, you're getting food everywhere.

ADNAN. Can't guess? You lose. Up against the wall!

IMM GHASSAN. Adnan!

ADNAN. Get up! Against the wall. No, wait. You by the oven, and you by the other oven. Zahra, stand on one leg. Hands behind your head.

ZAHRA. I'll fall! Please.

> IMM GHASSAN *doesn't get up, and takes hold of* ZAHRA *so she won't get up either.* ADNAN *gets up and pulls* ZAHRA, *who gives in and stands up.*

ADNAN (*to* ZAHRA). That's better. If you can't guess, you get punished. Get up, Imm Ghassan, let's play. No, hang on, you stay there. Because you're the mother, the originator of all this shit. If you don't guess it this time, I'll throw the food all over you. Food, oh yeah, I want some more. Why does the food taste like this? Your cooking's getting worse, Imm Ghassan. (*Goes to the fridge and gets more.*) The idiot was al-Tayyib. Son of that other idiot, Abu al-Tayyib. Ask me why.

ZAHRA. Why?

ADNAN. Because he's a moron. He nearly got us killed. We were in the room where I killed the guy. 'Run, run, they're bombing us.' When he was meant to be guarding us. So, we ran, and who was bombing us? (*Loudly.*) Who?

ZAHRA. The terrorists.

ADNAN (*going towards* ZAHRA, *pulling her by the ear*). How do they let you teach in a school? A bird-brain like you shouldn't be allowed to leave the house. Who has planes? Huh? Do the terrorists have planes, Imm Ghassan? Mother of Ghassan, the martyred pilot?

IMM GHASSAN *doesn't reply.*

That's right, clever girl. We were bombed by our own planes. Our planes. Our barrel bombs. (*To* IMM GHASSAN.) No big deal if we die by mistake, is it? (*To* ZAHRA.) No big deal, is it?

ZAHRA. It must have been a mistake.

ADNAN *slaps* ZAHRA.

ADNAN. That's so you don't make any mistakes! So you learn.

IMM GHASSAN (*furious*). Don't you dare lay a finger on her!

ADNAN. No, don't be angry at me.

He kisses the crying ZAHRA *in a way that frightens her.*

Is that better? Want me to kill you another one, for her?

IMM GHASSAN. Let her sit down.

ADNAN. If she guesses right next time, she can sit down. What happened to us then? Well, obviously we didn't die, did we? The house collapsed on us and we got trapped. The wall fell on Nabil's leg, al-Tayyib pissed himself and I got stuck with the guy I killed. There was no window, no door, no light, no air, nothing. No fucking mobile signal. And guess what else? If you guess right, I'll give you a treat before bed. But only if you brush your teeth. Have you been brushing the baby's teeth, Zahra?

IMM GHASSAN. Sit down, dear.

ADNAN. I'm the one that does the talking here. You can shut up!

IMM GHASSAN. What has she done?

ADNAN. What's she done? (*Imitating* ZAHRA.) Kill them, kill them. Get information out of them! Take pictures with them... Or don't you remember, Zuzu, what you said on the phone? How about I take a picture of you now, standing up to be punished?

ADNAN *comes very close to her, frightening her. He goes back to his food, guzzling it in a repulsive manner.* ZAHRA *bends to sit down.*

(*To* ZAHRA.) Up!

IMM GHASSAN. Sit down.

ADNAN. Sit the fuck down!

ZAHRA *cries and sits down.*

Sit closer to Mum. Next to each other. Good. So you understand better.

IMM GHASSAN *and* ZAHRA *move closer to one another.* ADNAN *gets up and climbs onto one of the appliances.*

After the bombing, me and Nabil and al-Tayyib are stuck in the room, white as ghosts from the dust we're covered in, and what comes down from here? From the ceiling?

IMM GHASSAN. Calm down, son. You're tired, darling, sit down. I know –

ADNAN. Let me finish! A little boy's hand appears. Seven years old maybe. Next, we see a bit of his body. Then his head comes down. And he just hangs there in the air, like he's being born! Covered in white sand. And his head's all red.

ZAHRA *screams, feels sick, runs to the side of the room and vomits.*

Well done, Zahra, well done! That's what al-Tayyib did. His mum, did she find out he burned to death?

IMM GHASSAN. She started wandering around outside, pulling her hair and swearing at everyone. Abu al-Tayyib won't let her out any more. She doesn't leave the house and he won't let anyone talk about it. Come on now, get down!

ADNAN. Do you know how al-Tayyib died? He died later, just like his father wanted. Not like Nabil, he died on the spot. His legs were hanging off and he was bleeding, but he was on TV, Zahra, wouldn't you like to be on telly? The presenter got to him in time and interviewed him while he was dying. Died live on TV. You know what fell off the boy?

IMM GHASSAN. Come down…

ADNAN *takes a gold chain from around his neck.*

ADNAN. And who's it a present for? For the baby… Zahra! Come here and take it.

ZAHRA *approaches and takes it from his hand.*

IMM GHASSAN. Zahra, put it away.

ADNAN. It's for the baby to wear.

IMM GHASSAN. It's bad luck, you shouldn't.

ADNAN (*laughs*). Don't you want him to be a martyr? Don't you love the martyrs? It's your fault, anyway. We're fighting a war you should have fought. If you'd just fought instead of being so spineless, we'd be alive now. Why did you delay it? Didn't you want to be martyrs? (*Pause.*) I swear to God I have no idea who I'm fighting for or against any more. I'm just defending myself. But when I get confused I get scared. And when I get scared I want to fight. When I fight, I regret it, maybe… And when I regret things I can't do anything. That makes me want to fight more so I don't regret anything. What would you do in my place?

SCENE THIRTEEN   97

ZAHRA. I don't know, love. I'd fight, like you.

ADNAN. Where are the clothes? The clothes I was wearing when I got here.

ZAHRA. I've hidden them... To have something that smells of you.

ADNAN. For when I die? Honestly, you're the cleverest one in the family. You should be headmistress – even that's not good enough for you.

ZAHRA. Do you want them?

ADNAN. No. Hide them somewhere good. Do you know whose clothes they are? Did you smell them properly?

ZAHRA *nods*.

And what did you think? They're the clothes of the guy I killed for Ghassan, so hide them somewhere safe.

ZAHRA *is dumbstruck*.

Your husband's a coward! His lot came in while we were still hiding in his house. I killed him, then put his clothes on, and I stayed alive!

IMM GHASSAN. It's okay, love. In war –

The goat comes in with a bell around its neck and a red ribbon around one of its legs.

ADNAN. Well, hello there! Look who's bored of sitting on their own.

ZAHRA *runs over to shoo it out*.

Leave it, leave it. Isn't that Ghassan? We were making so much noise! Couldn't you sleep? Poor thing! Have you seen what they did to us?

IMM GHASSAN. You should be ashamed of yourself.

ADNAN. You know, if you look hard, it kind of looks like him.

ZAHRA. Stop it, for God's sake, stop it!

ADNAN. I don't want to hear your voice.

ADNAN gets down, then gets on all fours and approaches the goat. IMM GHASSAN cries.

Why are you crying? Isn't he cute? Don't we look nice together? (*Bleating, like a goat.*) Is that good, or is my voice too low? Why isn't it answering me? I want a blue ribbon for my neck. When I turn into a goat will we be able to talk to each other?

IMM GHASSAN. Please get up, please!

ADNAN bleats, then goes over to his food, gets his plate, and puts it down for the goat, which starts to eat.

ADNAN. You're letting the poor thing go hungry! Look how it's eating. See, it likes your cooking.

IMM GHASSAN (*to ZAHRA*). Put it outside.

ADNAN. Is that how you're going to treat me?

IMM GHASSAN. God forbid!

ZAHRA. Of course not.

ADNAN (*laughs*). Get it out of here.

ADNAN turns to the food and pokes at it in disgust.

ZAHRA goes out with the goat. Pause. The sound of running water from the bathroom breaks the silence.

IMM GHASSAN. Take a deep breath and listen to me. You're going to leave the house before she's finished in the bathroom without saying a word, you're going to find the first smuggler you come across, and you're going to leave the country. Then you can phone me.

ADNAN puts out the candle out with his fingers. Darkness.

ADNAN. If you think I'm still a little boy, then you're a fool for sending a little boy to go and fight.

IMM GHASSAN. You should know by now how things work around here.

Pause.

ADNAN. I couldn't tell what you were going to say when I called
you. I spent thirty years living in this house, and I didn't know
what you'd say.

IMM GHASSAN. About what?

ADNAN (*angry*). I know the lines are tapped. But people
believe their own lies. When a father says to his son, 'I want
you to be a hero and make us proud.' It means, 'Go and die!'

IMM GHASSAN. People are scared of each other. People can't
even talk in their own homes. And that's why you need to
leave.

ADNAN. It's a bit late for that, Imm Ghassan. Two things you
can't stand in the way of – water rising, and people when
they rise up. Who told me that? Look at me!

IMM GHASSAN. The main thing is that you're safe.

ADNAN. Safe? I'm dead. You just can't see that.

   ADNAN *lights the candle*. IMM GHASSAN *gets up*,
   ADNAN *grabs her roughly by the arm*.

   You still haven't answered me.

IMM GHASSAN. No one knows who knows. No one knows
who doesn't know. No one knows anything. And no one can
say anything even if they do know. No one can be sure they
don't know. Some rumours were going around at one point,
then no one heard anything more. Everyone got scared, but
no one can say they're scared.

ADNAN. Surely you wondered why the boys started phoning
their families? Is that what soldiers normally do?

   IMM GHASSAN *exits*.

   ADNAN *pulls out his service-number chain from inside his
   shirt, and looks at it. Then* IMM GHASSAN *returns with
   a bag of food she has prepared in advance*.

IMM GHASSAN. You need to get out of the country.

ADNAN. Why didn't you leave ages ago? Why didn't you do
anything?

IMM GHASSAN. When you're older, you'll understand.

ADNAN. Stop avoiding the question. Tell me!

IMM GHASSAN. This isn't the time.

ADNAN. Why have kids, if we never see them or live with them?

IMM GHASSAN (*taking his face in her hands*). You're all
I have left!

ADNAN *grasps the service-number chain around his neck
and shows it to* IMM GHASSAN. *He then tucks it away
again.*

ADNAN. Make sure you memorise it.

IMM GHASSAN. Get out of here. Run away.

ADNAN. I might die before I find out if it's a boy or a girl. Or
who wins in the end.

IMM GHASSAN. Call me as soon as you're out of the country.

ADNAN. That day, why did you tell me to run away?

IMM GHASSAN. Abu Firas.

ADNAN. Do you know why?

IMM GHASSAN. I don't care, as long as you're here.

ADNAN. You don't mind spending the rest of your life like this?

IMM GHASSAN *remains silent.*

Get them to tell their sons to run away when they call. Or let
them not bother. Fuck them all.

ADNAN *exits, heading for the bathroom.*

IMM GHASSAN. Where are you going? (*Pause.*)

ZAHRA (*inside, screaming*). He's trying to kill the baby! He's
insane! Insane! Help!

IMM GHASSAN *turns on a light and runs to the screaming.*

The front door is heard closing.

Scene Fourteen – Killer

The space outside IMM GHASSAN*'s house. Night-time.*
ADNAN *comes out at a run.* ABU FIRAS *stops him.*

ABU FIRAS. I knew you'd come back. I was waiting for you.

ADNAN. You're still alive?

ABU FIRAS. They're watching me the whole time but they haven't killed me yet.

ADNAN. It won't be long, I'm sure.

ABU FIRAS. Tell me about Firas.

ADNAN. He's dead.

ABU FIRAS. Did you see him yourself?

ADNAN. You know everything.

ABU FIRAS. Not everything. Why do they call?

ADNAN. They capture us. Make us call you. You know that.

ABU FIRAS. Who's capturing who? I don't get it.

ADNAN. Hell. It's hell there.

ABU FIRAS. That I do know.

ADNAN. No, you don't. No one here has any idea. They fucking set up ambushes to capture us. I don't know, it's different every time, they capture one of us and make them call you, they make us talk to you, film us on their phones... And they make us ask you, while they're standing over us so we can hardly breathe.

ABU FIRAS. When Firas called me –

ADNAN. When I called they were breathing down my neck like wild animals. They were holding the phone and saying, ask your family. If I didn't make the call and ask, they were going to kill me. It's easy, repeat after me –

ABU FIRAS. 'I've caught some terrorists, what shall I do?'

ADNAN. 'I've caught some terrorists, what shall I do to them?'

ABU FIRAS (*horrified*). And what happens?

ADNAN. When I got caught, I was with al-Tayyib. We've
    escaped death twice, and we get caught again. Four men, with
    a boy of around twelve. He was listening to music on his
    mobile the whole time, I've still got one of the songs stuck in
    my head. One of them was in a fucking wedding dress.

ABU FIRAS. A wedding dress?

ADNAN. He'd been wearing it to fight, since our boys killed
    his fiancée. I thought it was all a laugh, a prank. I thought
    they were some of our lot, having a laugh. How was I meant
    to know? Turned out to be a trap. Fucking bastards. Same
    clothes as us. Same accent, even.

ABU FIRAS. What happened?

ADNAN. They took al-Tayyib first and made him call his moron
    of a father. Abu al-Tayyib goes, 'Burn them!' The second he
    got off the phone, one of them was shouting, 'Get the petrol!'
    I watched al-Tayyib burn to death before my eyes. They made
    Ramez dig his own grave. When I ran away, I could still hear
    him screaming as he was digging. (*Pause.*) Firas wasn't in my
    unit. But if he phoned you, then it was you that killed him.
    How did you want him to kill them?

    Pause.

ABU FIRAS. Why didn't you tell us what was happening?

ADNAN. None of us knew – until it happened to us.

    ABU FIRAS *breaks down.*

    Abu Firas, run away! Like you said to my mum to tell me.
    They'll kill you, I swear. When that lot get here. Or when
    people here find out you know. I bet you they know already.

ABU FIRAS. There's no way they know. They have to find out.

ADNAN. They won't believe you. Don't tell anyone... No, tell
    everyone! Let everyone in town find out. They'll go insane.
    They *should* go insane. Tell them not to send their kids to
    join the army. They'd be better off killing them.

ABU FIRAS. Why is this happening to us?

ADNAN (*grabbing hold of him*). Why is this happening to *us*?

> ADNAN *is about to run away, but* ABU FIRAS *catches hold of him*.

ABU FIRAS. Did I kill Firas?

ADNAN. Firas killed people too! That's how it works. You won't be able to change anything.

ABU FIRAS. Stay here, so they'll believe me.

ADNAN. If I say it, they'll kill me. Don't tell anyone you saw me. All the videos are online. (*Taking out his mobile phone*.) And here.

> ADNAN *starts playing one of the videos on his mobile, which we see on screen*.

> ABU FIRAS *grabs the phone immediately, aghast*. ADNAN *walks away*.

> ABU FIRAS *is left alone with the bleating of the goats*.

> *The sound of fighting is getting closer*.

Scene Fifteen – Burning coals

ABU AL-TAYYIB's house. The living room. We see the door to the kitchen and the front door. ABU AL-TAYYIB is smoking a hookah pipe and watching the official news, which we see on the screen. IMM AL-TAYYIB is sitting near him. Her long grey hair hangs over her face, and she is dipping a comb into a dish of water next to her and combing her hair, without showing her face. Every so often the goat bleats.

On screen, an advert comes on. A phone rings. A hand picks up the phone and places it to their ear, and a voice says, 'Don't sit at home being a disappointment to us all. Die for your country, and your family will receive a mountain goat.'

IMM AL-TAYYIB. Waiting for your interview?

ABU AL-TAYYIB. Do you know how many people died last year in traffic accidents because they were not wearing a seatbelt?

IMM AL-TAYYIB. No one owns a car any more.

ABU AL-TAYYIB. Is that what is important?

    MUDAR walks in through the front door, goes over to the sofa where ABU AL-TAYYIB is sitting, grabs his phone charger, and leaves. MUDAR comes back in through the front door, opens a cupboard and looks through it, then goes to search somewhere else. He finally finds some batteries, goes into the kitchen, then comes back huffing and tutting.

MUDAR. Don't we have any ice?

ABU AL-TAYYIB. I've told you lot to stop drinking.

IMM AL-TAYYIB (*from behind her hair*). Isn't there any left in the freezer?

MUDAR. No, or I wouldn't have asked.

    MUDAR exits. The news comes to an end.

IMM AL-TAYYIB. Leave it on for the weather.

    On the television, the weather forecast announces mild weather and sunshine for the following day.

ABU AL-TAYYIB. Have you seen who he is with?

IMM AL-TAYYIB (*from behind her hair*). Your nephew, Imm
    Suhayl's son, and Abu Ala''s son… It's lucky you used to be
    a TV presenter. My parents would not let me marry
    someone poor.

ABU AL-TAYYIB. Did you see his eyes?

IMM AL-TAYYIB (*uninterested*). No. If you were still
    presenting, could you avoid lying about the weather? You
    can change channels now.

ABU AL-TAYYIB. They have been smoking.

IMM AL-TAYYIB. We know that.

ABU AL-TAYYIB. Oh, that is all right then.

IMM AL-TAYYIB. We're not going to talk about it. His eyes
    are red because he is not sleeping. (*Pause.*) How can you sit
    there smoking when you're meant to be sad about your sons?

ABU AL-TAYYIB. Everyone has their own way of being sad.

IMM AL-TAYYIB. Do you think about them?

ABU AL-TAYYIB. What do you think?

IMM AL-TAYYIB. Can I cry, even if you won't?

    ABU AL-TAYYIB *doesn't reply.*

    You were upset about Zahra, weren't you?

ABU AL-TAYYIB. Why?

IMM AL-TAYYIB. She slipped in the bathroom. She is worried
    she'll have a miscarriage. The doctor told her to stay indoors.

ABU AL-TAYYIB. What's that got to do with us?

IMM AL-TAYYIB. You should let me out of the house to
    visit her.

ABU AL-TAYYIB. Oh, is she not teaching?

IMM AL-TAYYIB. You don't know anything.

ABU AL-TAYYIB. What are those bright sparks studying in the office then?

Pause.

IMM AL-TAYYIB. When we stop talking, the sound of the fighting is much clearer. Can you hear? It's getting closer.

ABU AL-TAYYIB. You stopped talking? I didn't notice.

IMM AL-TAYYIB. Anyway, they're better off here in the office, where we can keep an eye. And it's a good influence for them to be in the Party Office.

ABU AL-TAYYIB. You must be joking. They have turned it into a cabaret...

IMM AL-TAYYIB *laughs*.

I don't see what is so funny.

IMM AL-TAYYIB. You. Let's not give al-Tayyib's room to the goat.

ABU AL-TAYYIB. No one suggested that.

IMM AL-TAYYIB. The goat is giving Mudar an allergy. (*Pause.*) I want to go back to work.

ABU AL-TAYYIB (*ruminating*). They are not normal cigarettes, you know.

(*To* IMM AL-TAYYIB.) We talked about you working. (*Thinking.*) Not just cigarettes.

IMM AL-TAYYIB. Next, you'll tell me they've got girls in there... Put yourself in my position. If they kicked you out of the Party, what would you do?

ABU AL-TAYYIB. What do you mean?

IMM AL-TAYYIB. Wouldn't you be worried about being unemployed? They gave Abu Karim the heave-ho one night, without so much as a word of warning.

ABU AL-TAYYIB. Abu Karim made an unforgivable mistake. Abu Karim failed to do his job properly.

IMM AL-TAYYIB. Anyone can make a mistake. And no one knows when they're going to. No one knows what's suddenly going to be considered a mistake. It'll be right today and then suddenly wrong tomorrow. Wrong... Anyway, like you don't know who wrote the report about him! A mistake... I heard you all talking, I know you well. I'll put a wash on tomorrow. I have so much washing to do. If the weather is fine tomorrow, will they be bringing martyrs to the square?

ABU AL-TAYYIB. Oh, give it a rest.

IMM AL-TAYYIB. Well, if it rains they'll get wet. It would be a shame. (*Pause*.) Do you think it really will be dry tomorrow like it said? Sometimes they get the forecast right by accident. Will the martyrs be buried or will they float back up to the surface? (*Pause*.) Well, if they're going to bring the martyrs then why shouldn't I do the washing, even if it does rain? Yes, that's what I'm going to do!

ABU AL-TAYYIB. Don't. Kinan and al-Tayyib's clothes don't need washing.

IMM AL-TAYYIB. They're dirty.

ABU AL-TAYYIB. They're clean.

IMM AL-TAYYIB. They're dirty.

ABU AL-TAYYIB. You've just washed them. You wash them every few days.

IMM AL-TAYYIB. Say it!

ABU AL-TAYYIB. I'm not saying anything.

IMM AL-TAYYIB. Say it. It's fine.

ABU AL-TAYYIB. Let's take care of the idiot we've got left as much as well –

IMM AL-TAYYIB. As what?

ABU AL-TAYYIB. You know, don't act stupid.

IMM AL-TAYYIB. As the ones we lost.

ABU AL-TAYYIB. Couldn't you smell it?!

IMM AL-TAYYIB. His clothes are clean! (*Pause*.) Aren't you worried there'll come a day when you just can't do it any more?

ABU AL-TAYYIB. I can't put up with you any more.

IMM AL-TAYYIB. I want to go and see my family.

ABU AL-TAYYIB. No one is stopping you.

IMM AL-TAYYIB. For once. Are you going to send me with a chaperone?

ABU AL-TAYYIB. Yes, or you will embarrass us.

IMM AL-TAYYIB. When will they take away the cemetery?

ABU AL-TAYYIB. No one is taking anything.

IMM AL-TAYYIB. I heard. They are building a mall over the cemetery. When is it going to happen? I will have to buy my father from the shopping mall.

ABU AL-TAYYIB. That's enough! Stop listening when I am on the phone. You should be ashamed.

   Pause.

IMM AL-TAYYIB. Do dead bodies really get eaten by worms?

   ABU AL-TAYYIB *ignores this*.

   Mum might ask about Kinan. I didn't even tell her about al-Tayyib.

   He doesn't reply.

   Has my mother been eaten by worms? The goats are shitting there. They must be shitting on my mother.

   ABU AL-TAYYIB *doesn't reply*.

   Apparently, goatshit worms are good for the soil. Why is that?

ABU AL-TAYYIB. They are like fertiliser.

IMM AL-TAYYIB. How can you be so sure?

ABU AL-TAYYIB. Of what?

IMM AL-TAYYIB. Of everything. (*Gets up and exits to the kitchen.*) Leave them alone in the office. Don't shout at Mudar. He wets himself at night.

ABU AL-TAYYIB *returns with charcoal for the hookah pipe.*

ABU AL-TAYYIB. They finished the vodka. (*Adjusts the charcoal on the pipe.*)

IMM AL-TAYYIB. Apparently, his Excellency-the-President's wife is going to personally congratulate the woman who is mother to the most martyrs. Maybe we should have had more children. (*Thinks.*) Are you scared *for* them, or scared *of* them?

He does not reply.

Respect or contempt?

ABU AL-TAYYIB. Bullshit!

IMM AL-TAYYIB. Maybe also... (*Pause.*) Question: do I love you at all? I need money.

ABU AL-TAYYIB. You've got money.

IMM AL-TAYYIB. No I haven't.

ABU AL-TAYYIB. Did you burn it again?

IMM AL-TAYYIB. I don't like fire.

ABU AL-TAYYIB. I put it next to the microwave for you.

IMM AL-TAYYIB. You know I don't go near it.

ABU AL-TAYYIB. Did you take it?

ABU AL-TAYYIB (*gets a call, answers the phone, and listens to what is said. To the caller*). Mmm. Hmm. Right. (*Hangs up, looking uncomfortable.*)

IMM AL-TAYYIB. Does Kinan have enough money? (*Thinks.*) You've started screaming in your sleep.

Loud raps at the door. ABU AL-TAYYIB *gets up.* ABU
AL-TAYYIB *looks through the peephole.* IMM AL-TAYYIB
*raises her head, leaving her hair to hang down her back.
We see her face. She picks up the remote which* ABU
AL-TAYYIB *has left behind, and flicks through the channels
looking for something entertaining.*

ABU AL-TAYYIB. Go inside!

IMM AL-TAYYIB. I am inside.

ABU AL-TAYYIB *is forced to open the door to put a stop to
the deafening banging.*

ABU FIRAS *enters angrily and immediately slaps* ABU
AL-TAYYIB *around the face.* ABU AL-TAYYIB *is stunned.*
IMM AL-TAYYIB *laughs.*

ABU AL-TAYYIB (*to* IMM AL-TAYYIB). Get out!

IMM AL-TAYYIB *exits and goes into the kitchen. Two*
BODYGUARDS *arrive in a hurry.* ABU AL-TAYYIB
gestures to them to go.

Silence.

It might not be the first time, but it is certainly the last.

ABU FIRAS. Criminal!

ABU AL-TAYYIB. Keep your voice down, the boys are in the
office. Don't make me have the bodyguards tie you up in
front of them.

ABU FIRAS. You knew about the phone calls, and you said
nothing?

ABU AL-TAYYIB. I have no idea what you are talking about.

ABU FIRAS. Liar!

ABU AL-TAYYIB. I never lie.

ABU FIRAS. I can show you videos to jog your memory. They
are all over the internet.

ABU AL-TAYYIB (*realising how much* ABU FIRAS *knows*).
Abu Firas, you poor thing.

ABU FIRAS. How can you kill your own son and stand in front
of me now? How will you be able to go to his grave? Now
I see why you wouldn't open the coffins. You didn't want me
to know.

ABU AL-TAYYIB. I don't know… I don't know what you're
talking about.

ABU FIRAS. That's not an answer. If you don't tell me, I'm
going to go around showing the videos to the whole village.

ABU AL-TAYYIB. Go on then!

  ABU FIRAS *is taken aback*.

  Why, weren't you expecting that? Aren't you talking about
  the phone calls? If you think people are going to believe all
  those fake videos, you're mistaken. Do you think we'd let
  ourselves be tricked by some lie made up by the opposition?
  My dear teacher, at the next Party meeting we will show
  them how the videos are made to weaken our boys' resolve.
  How it is all a bunch of lies. We can always find an answer.
  So, show them to anyone you like.

ABU FIRAS. They'll never believe that.

ABU AL-TAYYIB. We've done it before and you all went
along with it.

ABU FIRAS. You can't keep lying to people forever.

ABU AL-TAYYIB. Who said it was a lie? People hear what
they want to hear. It is a shame.

ABU FIRAS. Lies always get found out in the end.

ABU AL-TAYYIB. If it does get found out, it will only be to
cover up for another one. Wake up, Abu Firas. You're in the
war. If the sound of fighting seems a long way off, that just
means it's going to get closer.

ABU FIRAS. You knew that you were sending your son to his
death.

ABU AL-TAYYIB. That is not true.

ABU FIRAS. You knew, before he called. You knew, before our sons called us, and you didn't tell us.

ABU AL-TAYYIB. Why do you care so much about my answer?

Enter IMM AL-TAYYIB, *who has heard everything, in a state of shock. She freezes, unable to scream. Then she begins to let out unearthly, animal shrieks, pulling her hair and slapping her head as she screams. She turns to* ABU AL-TAYYIB's *hookah pipe, grabs the pieces of charcoal, rubs them into her hair and begins to scream.* ABU AL-TAYYIB *runs over to her, flabbergasted at what she is doing, and tries to put a stop to her fit of hysteria. He puts his arms around her in an attempt to get her to be quiet and to take the coals from her.*

ABU FIRAS *remains rooted to the spot.*

Shhh, be quiet! Let go! (*To* ABU FIRAS.) Happy?

IMM AL-TAYYIB *begins to throw the coals she is holding at* ABU AL-TAYYIB, *who tries to hold his tongue and not shout, while dodging the hot coals.*

IMM AL-TAYYIB. You knew, you criminal. You're a criminal. I hate fire.

ABU AL-TAYYIB. None of it is true.

ABU FIRAS. You refuse to believe it.

IMM AL-TAYYIB. What difference does it make? You would have done the same thing anyway. You are a criminal. You're vile. Vile.

ABU FIRAS. You knew? How long have you known?

ABU AL-TAYYIB (*to* IMM AL-TAYYIB). Abu Firas is insane! Don't listen to him. (*To* ABU FIRAS.) You cannot change anything.

IMM AL-TAYYIB. You're a criminal. The poor things. Poor things. Are you scared? Scared of them? What could make you kill your own son? Nothing. You are vile, vile. And you killed your son. My son.

ABU AL-TAYYIB. I did not kill him. Al-Tayyib died a martyr.
Al-Tayyib was fighting in a war. Soldiers have to lay down
their lives in war. That's it, that's what war is.
(*To* ABU FIRAS.) *You* should have been buried first.

IMM AL-TAYYIB. When he called us, the poor thing wanted
our help. He did *not* want to die... You killed him. 'Burn
them.' You could have said anything. Fire. Coals.

ABU AL-TAYYIB. Al-Tayyib knows. Al-Tayyib understands.
Al-Tayyib is a hero.

ABU AL-TAYYIB *tries to overpower* IMM AL-TAYYIB.
ABU FIRAS *stands watching*.

*A goat is bleating nearby. From the office, filters in the sound
of* TEENAGERS' *laughs*.

Scene Sixteen – Game

The Party Office. MUDAR, SAMI *and* JUDE *are drinking
vodka and watching television (the screen). They flick though
the channels. sports, action films, music videos, cartoons.
In front of them is a pile of textbooks, schoolbooks, and pens,
and a laptop, which* JUDE *is playing on.* JUDE *is rolling a
joint.* MUDAR *is adroitly taking apart an M16 gun to clean it,
then putting it back together. He cleans it using the brightly
coloured fabric which he fetched from the house in the last
scene. When he finishes putting it back together, he amuses
himself by taking aim at the others at whim, for the things they
say.* SAMI *is absorbed in his phone.*

Enter FADI, *returning from the toilet, doing up his flies.*

JUDE (*pointing to* FADI's *crotch*). Anything in there?

FADI. Fuck off.

JUDE. Alright, can't you take a joke?

FADI *sits down*. JUDE *lights the joint and they pass it around. Pause.*

FADI. I'm bored.

JUDE. Got anything better we could be doing at a shitty time like this?

FADI. Something new. Anything. I'll do anything.

SAMI. Leave the country?

FADI. Wouldn't you?

MUDAR. My dad would lose his shit…

JUDE. Go and blow yourself up, it'd be better than drowning. Either you're locked up here, or you're a soldier posted at some godforsaken checkpoint, or you drown attempting to escape and they fish you out by the tail and drag you back like a rat. Or you can stay here and wank in the bathroom. Those are your options.

SAMI *and* MUDAR *laugh.*

Do you really want to do something fun? Something you haven't done before?

FADI. If this is a joke, you can spare me.

JUDE. Get up! (*Makes a sexual gesture, then twists a Coca-Cola metal tag right and left.*) He can. He can't. He can. He can't. He can. He can't.

FADI (*annoyed, to* SAMI). Just a sec. He'd better explain what he's on about, or I'll put out this joint in his face.

MUDAR. Aww, got your period?

SAMI. To be fair, every day's the same. The same, the same, the same, the same, the same, the same…

FADI (*pushing away the gun*). Get that fucking thing out of my face when you're talking.

JUDE. So, if Miss has a miscarriage, do we still have to go to school?

SAMI. They know there's a war on. At least they can let us enjoy these few years, fucking cunts. No school for me thanks. I mean, what would happen?

JUDE. What's the point of going to school if we're only going to join the army?

FADI. Early starts and homework and shit like that... What's the point?

SAMI. Isn't it weird?

FADI. If we stay here, we'll have to join the army in a few years. I don't want to.

JUDE. Dude, didn't you hear what his dad said? You can sign up already.

MUDAR. Won't it be over, by the time it's our turn?

JUDE. Like hell it will.

SAMI. If things stay like this, I'm signing up. I'm not going to wait around.

MUDAR. No one's stopping you. Firas just went, he didn't sit here talking shit about it.

JUDE. I wanna fight too. Bam bam bam! Catch the bastards. Ha, take that, ha! I'm not going to stand at some checkpoint looking at IDs and going through chicks' handbags.

FADI. Well, you don't need to worry about dying. You're worth a whole goat!

JUDE. And you're not worth shit. You know, you really remind me of Yazan, God rest his soul. I couldn't stand him.

SAMI. Coward. I didn't even know his name before he died.

JUDE (*to* SAMI). Take me with you!

SAMI. Next time, but it's not a game. Real people, real shooting. Not like PlayStation. Where do they come from, man? Out of the ground, out of trees, out of the sky... It's unreal, it's like – they don't get tired.

MUDAR. They give them pills.

FADI. They give our lot pills too.

JUDE. We'll show them. I'd chop one of their hearts out and eat it with my bare hands... Why does this hash taste weird?

SAMI. It's all there is, so you'd better get used to it.

MUDAR. Tastes like hospitals and nurses.

SAMI. Sick! Now, who does that remind me of?

FADI. I'm going to leave. Might be another ten years of this. There's things I want to do.

JUDE. It's not that hard. You're just not man enough!

FADI *lunges towards* JUDE *and starts punching him.* JUDE *squares up to him, mockingly.* FADI *twists* JUDE*'s arm, catching him by surprise.* JUDE *laughs derisively, sure that* FADI *isn't capable of hurting him.* SAMI *and* MUDAR *step forward and join in punching him, jokingly moving closer to his crotch area.* JUDE *defends himself, laughing, and fights* FADI. *The others don't attempt to pull them apart.* MUDAR *aims the gun at each of them in turn.*

Light knocks at the door. ABU AL-TAYYIB *enters without waiting for a response.* FADI, *embarrassed, stops punching* JUDE, *who straightens out his appearance. They are flustered and quickly stub out their joints and cigarettes.*

ABU AL-TAYYIB. How are we doing, boys?

MUDAR. Hi, Dad. What's up?

FADI. Hi, Uncle. Come in.

ABU AL-TAYYIB. Mudar, son, haven't you put that away yet?

MUDAR. I've only just finished cleaning it.

ABU AL-TAYYIB. We have to set a good example. The last thing we want to hear is that Abu al-Tayyib's son was playing with –

MUDAR. I'll put it back now.

ABU AL-TAYYIB. Don't be upset with me now! We're all friends here. Anyway, I'm not just talking about you. I mean all of you young men. You're not just our children... You're the nation's arsenal.

MUDAR *cringes.*

Did I say something wrong?

MUDAR. No, but you know... I'm hanging out with the guys, and you –

ABU AL-TAYYIB. And I'm being boring again and lecturing you.

SAMI. Don't say that, Uncle. We're used to it.

ABU AL-TAYYIB. I was a young man, just like you lot once. I know what it's like! Do you think we didn't get up to the same things when we were your age? We got up to much worse. We did things none of you could do, you lot are nothing compared to the boys in our day.

JUDE. Was there a war on then?

ABU AL-TAYYIB. Does there have to be a war on for us to be prepared? That's the difference between our generation and yours... Anyway, I'll leave you to it for a bit before you head home. And thank you for all your hard work for the Party over the last few days. After the statue's been unveiled tomorrow there'll be no need for it to be guarded any more. Mudar, can I have you for a minute? (*Decides to say one more thing before leaving.*) And, boys – a little bit of alcohol and tobacco now and then is good fun. But go easy on it. It's not nice for me to keep saying this. Of course, I understand you want to unwind. But you're overdoing it. Don't think you can pull the wool over my eyes. I can smell everything, and I know what it all is.

They smile ingratiatingly.

Give my best to your parents. See you all tomorrow.

No sooner does MUDAR *make a move to leave with* ABU AL-TAYYIB *than the laptop suddenly makes a noise:*

a woman moaning. They are mortified. JUDE *hurriedly attempts to stop it, but fails. The sound goes on for a few more seconds before he manages to mute it.*

Honestly, there is no hope for us.

MUDAR *leaves with him. Pause.*

SAMI. Is he kicking us out?

JUDE. You never know what he's trying to say. He never just comes out and says it.

FADI. He's saying, we should go home before he kicks us out.

JUDE. He always has to make out like he needs something so he can come in here and see what we're up to. So fucking sly! And they think we don't know why.

FADI. Do you think he's going to tell him off because of the noise?

JUDE. It's a shame, man, it was cool sitting up there by the statue at night.

FADI. Oh, come on, hardly.

SAMI. What gets to me is how they never mention Kinan. I bet you anything he's saying something about him now.

JUDE. It's like he never existed. How do they do it?

SAMI. Loads of families do it. I dunno, it's like they're trained.

JUDE. I mean we spend every evening round their house and we can't ask about their son. Isn't it weird not to ask, you know, 'Where's your son got to all of a sudden, Uncle?' Everyone knows he left. It's only them that don't know that we know.

FADI. Why do you want to ask, if you already know?

JUDE. To find out if he drowned, or got killed, or got arrested.

FADI. Why don't they send Mudar away?

JUDE. His mum would lose it.

SAMI. What, like she isn't nuts already?

FADI. I heard Kinan ran away, joined the Free Army...

JUDE. Free Army, my arse. No way.

Pause.

FADI. Guys, do you know anything about the phone thing that's going on?

JUDE. No one's sure of anything.

SAMI. What's this? I haven't heard about it.

FADI. Oh, come on. You all know something weird's going on. Didn't you hear –

JUDE (*interrupting*). Where do you get this stuff? It's all a hoax, they make it up to scare us.

SAMI. There's all kinds of weird stories going around, doesn't mean any of it is true.

FADI. Try looking it up. Have a look at some of the blocked sites, then come and talk to me.

JUDE. What, you go on opposition websites?

FADI. What, you've never been on them?

SAMI. Oh, give it a rest before I block your face.

JUDE. No fucking chance I'd believe anything they write. You're a fucking fool if you read shit like that.

FADI. This is unreal, you can't even say anything to your own friends any more.

JUDE. You can't even know who your friends are any more!

SAMI. You'll get arrested. The whole internet is under surveillance, you stupid dick.

FADI. I'm going to get out of here. Like Adnan. And everyone else.

JUDE. Adnan's gone?

SAMI. Hasn't he gone back to the front?

JUDE. So, Miss Zahra is available.

FADI. She wants to break up with him, apparently.

MUDAR returns.

JUDE. What did he want?

MUDAR. To finish off his lecture.

FADI. Did you get ice?

MUDAR. There's none left.

JUDE. Ask your mum.

MUDAR. She's too busy brushing her hair for the millionth time today.

MUDAR hands the batteries and the charger to SAMI.

FADI. He's run out of juice.

They laugh. SAMI puts his mobile on to charge then takes out a plastic toy – a soldier lying down on his front carrying a gun. He puts in the batteries, and puts it down on the ground.

MUDAR. That's what you're getting so horny about?

They watch the soldier for a while. MUDAR goes back to holding the gun. The plastic soldier crawls on its stomach between their legs, emitting a tinny, irritating gunfire sound.

JUDE. Seriously though, what did he say?

FADI. Why do you care?

MUDAR. They're coming to film something tomorrow.

SAMI. I'm not leaving the house, I don't care who's been killed, I want to see the rerun of El Clasico!

JUDE. The presenter's hot, we should go and see if she's got her legs out. (*To* MUDAR.) And if your dad's checking her out.

SAMI. Is your dad having a thing with her?

MUDAR. Fuck off.

SAMI. He's having a thing with her.

FADI. What are they filming?

MUDAR. They've caught some terrorists and they want to film their confessions.

FADI. What, they've caught terrorists here? They've got this far?

MUDAR. And there's a foreign delegation coming for a few days, for a big celebration. They're planning something spontaneous.

SAMI *picks up the plastic soldier, which has got stuck by the sofa, watches it crawling in mid-air for a moment, then places it back down on the floor.*

JUDE. What – foreigners, here? Are they bringing any chicks with them?

MUDAR. They're coming to collect seeds. We have really special vegetables. Apparently because the soil is so fertile. They want to save them from extinction in case anything happens.

FADI. What about me?

JUDE. Turn into a seed and they'll let you out. They'd probably put you in a museum too.

They laugh. MUDAR *aims the gun at* JUDE, *then at* FADI *while he's talking.* MUDAR *makes a noise like he's shot* FADI. FADI *pretends to die.* JUDE *goes to the bathroom.*

SAMI. Who's down to get a tattoo?

MUDAR. What?

SAMI. Apparently, they bring a guy to do tattoos for the soldiers for free. I'm going to go and get one done too.

FADI. I'm going to head home.

MUDAR. I'm dying to get one. What are you going to get?

SAMI. Have to check if the guy knows how to do anything other than Party slogans and pictures of the President's face first!

They laugh.

JUDE (*just returned*). Guys, when I was looking at it in the loo, I was thinking, we can't let you go home before you've had a bit of fun!

FADI. Suck my dick!

JUDE. No thanks.

SAMI. What are you going to do at home?

JUDE. Go on the internet... (*Mimes masturbation.*)

SAMI. Stay here, we'll help you with that.

FADI *gets up and heads for the door.*

JUDE. If you were a real man you'd tap that.

MUDAR (*sniggering*). God, you're disgusting.

SAMI. Is it a he or a she?

FADI. Who are you on about?

JUDE. What, you've got no idea?

SAMI. Hmm, who's he going to fuck? Mudar's mum? Your cousin? My cousin? Your aunt? We're all related...

They laugh, mocking him. FADI *comes over and grabs* JUDE *by his clothes.*

FADI. Don't make me lose my shit.

JUDE. If you're a man, go and fuck the goat outside.

FADI *lets go of him while the others laugh smugly.*

SAMI. Man, that's a genius idea.

JUDE. If you know how to fuck, that is. If you can even get it up.

FADI. Oh, for fuck's sake, I've had enough of this.

MUDAR. You two are disgusting.

JUDE. When was the last time you used it? We should make sure it's doing all right.

SAMI. He sorts himself out.

MUDAR. Where do you get girls from, anyway?

JUDE. If you weren't so scared of your dad, you'd have come with us and stood at the school gates.

MUDAR. Not my kind of thing.

JUDE. Doesn't have to be girls. In the army, loads of them fuck goats... It's well known.

FADI. Okay, enough, before I –

SAMI. Let's hope your dad doesn't walk in and hear us.

JUDE (*mockingly*). I'm sure it's crossed his mind. He was such a stud when he was a teenager, remember.

They laugh.

MUDAR. Leave my dad out of it, okay?

SAMI. Hey, no one said there was anything wrong with it. He has to learn how to fuck.

MUDAR. Okay, guys, chill out. Stop taking the piss.

JUDE. I'm not. I literally think he should fuck the goat.

SAMI. Why don't you go first, show him how it's done? I mean, he might not know how.

FADI. There's an idea.

JUDE. I'm happy with what I've got, and happy with what I'm fucking. I'm not looking for anything new.

FADI. Oh, 'new', is it? Like you've never tried.

JUDE (*trying not to get too annoyed*). Fuck off!

MUDAR. He's only joking.

FADI. No, I'm serious. Let him show me how to fuck a goat, and I'm happy to go after him. Then we'll see who's the real man.

SAMI. Poor thing, this beast might hurt her.

MUDAR (*annoyed*). Come on, guys. Just go home.

FADI. I'm not leaving until your friend tells us who's the real man around here.

MUDAR. Okay, okay, you're the man. Just give us a break. Come on.

> JUDE *looks* FADI *in the eye.* JUDE *unbuckles his belt and pulls it out of the belt loops.* MUDAR *mutes the screen.*

Chill the fuck out, guys! You must be joking.

> JUDE *opens the door and leaves.* SAMI, MUDAR *and* FADI *follow him. Muffled laughs come from outside.*

VOICE OF SAMI. What if his dick gets stuck in it?

VOICE OF MUDAR. He'll have to bring it with him to the burial tomorrow.

VOICE OF SAMI. No fucking way, man. He's actually going to do it.

> *The guffaws get louder. Pause.*

Look, there's someone waving over there. A soldier in a wedding dress.

VOICE OF MUDAR. It must be a crazy person... What's he doing in the middle of the night?

VOICE OF SAMI. Doesn't look like he's from around here.

VOICE OF FADI. Will it get pregnant?

VOICE OF JUDE. Who's the man, then?

> *Laughter mingles with the sound of* IMM AL-TAYYIB's *shrieking from upstairs. The bleating of the goat is very loud.*

VOICE OF FADI. Isn't that your mum screaming?

Inside the room, the screen makes white noise. The toy soldier continues to crawl across the floor.

Scene Seventeen – Lesson

The school. Night-time. ABU FIRAS *opens the door and enters, pulling the goat behind him. He turns on the light but the room remains dim. He ties the goat to a chair. He wipes the board and slowly writes on it the following: 'HISTORY. Repeats Itself. PERIOD. Final. SUBJECT. The Past. TOPIC. The Future.' He begins to write on the board. Lights down.*

The school bell rings and the voices of ZAHRA *and the* PUPILS *approach the door from outside. At the moment the door is opened, the stage lights go up. It is morning. We see* ABU FIRAS *hanging from the classroom ceiling. He has hung himself using the goat's tether. The goat hangs in mid-air, gasping weakly. The sight of* ABU FIRAS *is horrifying. He has urinated on himself.*

ZAHRA *screams, as do the* PUPILS, *many of whom recoil in fright and run from the room.* ZAHRA *hurriedly closes the door so no one can enter.* FADI, JUDE, SAMI, MUDAR *and a handful of other* PUPILS *remain with* ZAHRA. *They are upset and agitated.* ZAHRA *is at a loss as to what to do and feels nauseous. She is still pregnant.* SAMI *helps her sit down.*

On the board is written: 'I remained silent about my crimes against others and thus I killed my son. This is the fate of every man who stays silent. Firas called me for help from an ambush with opposition fighters, and what I wanted done to them was done to him. I sentenced him to death. We have all killed our children through our ignorance and fear. Now every fallen fighter is my son. We are eating each other's flesh. It is only the poor who die, and the regime, who are directing this war, do not attempt to stand up to or stop this machine, only to benefit from it. Do not go to war for it will not build a better nation. Doubt, questioning, courage. This is my final lesson.'

ZAHRA. Close your eyes. Somebody phone the headmaster. No, someone phone Comrade Abu al-Tayyib. Nobody say anything to anyone outside. Don't let anyone in. Until we know… Don't worry. You can go. No – no one leave!

SAMI. Miss, Mudar is calling his dad now.

MUDAR *steps aside to call his father.* ZAHRA *cries.* FADI *takes some photos of* ABU FIRAS *and the blackboard with his phone.*

FADI. Killed himself…

SAMI. Obviously…

ZAHRA. Quiet.

SAMI. Fine.

JUDE. Miss, hasn't he killed himself?

ZAHRA. What does it look like to you?

FADI. Miss, have you seen what's written on the board?

ZAHRA *turns to look, but she sees* ABU FIRAS *again and shrinks back.* FADI *starts to cry.*

SAMI. Can't you see she's not up to it?

FADI. Should we do something?

MUDAR. He's here.

JUDE. Miss, if you're not feeling well, I'll take you home.

ZAHRA. No.

FADI. What's happening?

ABU AL-TAYYIB *enters without knocking and takes in the ghastly scene in front of him. He is unshaven and has visible burn marks. In shock, he walks around* ABU FIRAS.

ABU AL-TAYYIB. No… No… Lord help us… May God have mercy on your soul, Abu Firas. What have they done to you?

MUDAR. Who, Dad?

ABU AL-TAYYIB. Miss Comrade, I am so sorry. All of you. This is the last thing I expected, even though… I expected it. What a loss this is.

ZAHRA. Comrade, we came in and –

ABU AL-TAYYIB. You don't need to say any more. It is all too clear. (*To* MUDAR.) Mudar, son, why did you tell me that he killed himself? Abu Firas was murdered. This is the work of armed terrorist gangs. A respectable man like Abu Firas would never commit suicide.

ZAHRA. Murdered!

MUDAR, SAMI *and* FADI *make a move to take* ABU FIRAS'*s body down*.

ABU AL-TAYYIB. Leave him, boys. Nobody touch anything until the police get here.

JUDE. I told you.

ABU AL-TAYYIB. Please, do not look at him any more – for the sake of his dignity, as our teacher. (*To* MUDAR.) It is pandemonium out there, thanks to your classmates who left. So we need your help.

MUDAR. But –

ABU AL-TAYYIB. That suicide story you gave me was obviously a mistaken first impression. The leadership were aware that Abu Firas had received threats, but we mistakenly thought he was safe. No word of this will leave this room. The classroom is a sacred space of learning, and everything that takes place within it remains within it. There will be no leaks – no WhatsApp, no Facebook, nothing of that sort. This is a big responsibility, when you are still so young. But you are men, you can do it.

MUDAR. What?

SAMI. Of course.

Pause.

ABU AL-TAYYIB. What did we see?

JUDE (*raising his hand for permission to speak*). But comrade, sir, how would armed terrorists have got into the village in the middle of the night just like that?

MUDAR. That's really scary!

JUDE. Could they murder someone in their home, then bring them to the school?

ZAHRA *awaits* ABU AL-TAYYIB*'s response attentively.*

ABU AL-TAYYIB. Listen, son. We are surrounded by collaborators. By rats, by germs. They are recruited from our ranks. That's why we ask people to report any strange behaviour. This is an immense conspiracy.

ZAHRA. Comrade, someone must have got in to carry out the operation.

ABU AL-TAYYIB. Yes, and snuck away like a cockroach!

SAMI. Comrade, they used the goat to kill him.

ZAHRA. Yes! Something to do with what was going on.

ABU AL-TAYYIB. Almost certainly, comrade.

SAMI. So, sir. Maybe he was in contact with the opposition, and they killed him?

JUDE. Have we been infiltrated, comrade, sir?

ABU AL-TAYYIB. Now, your teacher is hanging in the air. Let us hear no more of this now. We should think about defending our village, not panic about infiltrators.

FADI. But sir, on the board, I know it from class – that is his handwriting. Isn't it, Mudar?

MUDAR *agrees.* ABU AL-TAYYIB *notices the words written on the board and becomes angry. He walks slowly over to wipe the board clean as he speaks.*

ABU AL-TAYYIB. Incredible! They even imitate his handwriting – and write inflammatory messages in his name.

FADI. But sir, that is his handwriting. You can see his marks in my exercise book...

ABU AL-TAYYIB. Son, they could dictate it, and force him to write it. Couldn't they?

FADI (*gesturing to the board, where the writing was*). Like the phone calls, sir.

ABU AL-TAYYIB *is irritated at this. He has finished wiping the board.*

ZAHRA. Don't be silly! What are you talking about?

ABU AL-TAYYIB. Weak minds are being influenced by this madness. I can't believe one of our men-of-the-future would fall for this absurdity.

JUDE. Sir, Miss is tired. Do you want –

ABU AL-TAYYIB. Before you leave, look carefully at the board. Your teacher. Is that his handwriting? Is what was written there believable?

JUDE. No, definitely not...

SAMI. Even if he had been –

ABU AL-TAYYIB. Even if.

SAMI. Like you were saying, comrade.

FADI. Yeah, they could have forced him to write it...

ABU AL-TAYYIB *scrutinises them carefully.*

MUDAR. Will the goat be all right like that?

ABU AL-TAYYIB. Son, that is enough chit-chat. (*To* MUDAR.) Mudar, tell the Head to evacuate the school immediately.

The TEENAGERS *head for the door.*

Excuse me, we'll say the *fatiha* before we leave.

The TEENAGERS *are embarrassed at their blunder. Under* ABU AL-TAYYIB*'s watchful gaze, they recite the* fatiha, *and then leave.* ABU AL-TAYYIB *surveys* ABU FIRAS *and the goat in incredulity.* ZAHRA *looks about, confused and anxious.* ABU AL-TAYYIB *notices. Pause.*

To be honest, I am shocked. Despite everything... May he rest in peace.

ZAHRA. What do you mean, comrade?

ABU AL-TAYYIB. Look what he did – he tied the rope, around and around. So there was no way he could change his mind.

ZAHRA *is flustered and confused.* ABU AL-TAYYIB *drags over a chair to climb up and bring down* ABU FIRAS.

Now, Comrade Zahra. Let me tell you what you are thinking. 'Abu Firas killed himself, but why Abu al-Tayyib doesn't see that?' Answer me.

ZAHRA. Comrade, only before you arrived... But your explanation, it is convincing and –

ABU AL-TAYYIB. And you are one of us, one of our brightest young talents. We will rely on you in the future. You must be clever. Look at me, and tell me what you think happened.

ZAHRA *stays silent.*

You saw it with your own eyes. Abu Firas killed himself, that seems to be the evidence. Watch me carefully. I undo the rope. And you tell yourself that Abu Firas was murdered. (*Pause.*) Comrade, why did Abu Firas kill himself?

ZAHRA. I don't know if he did kill himself.

ABU AL-TAYYIB. Why do you not know?

ZAHRA *looks more flustered.*

Abu Firas killed himself... But what for?

ZAHRA *is silent.*

Firas's death. And why did Firas die, comrade? Who killed Firas?

ZAHRA *starts to cry.*

Do not cry. Firas is a martyr. Firas died fighting terrorists. The terrorists killed Abu Firas's son. His son – the dearest thing anyone can possess. (*Pause.*) Then the terrorists convinced him that he'd killed his own son. That's why he wanted to open the coffin to make sure. The terrorists killed Abu Firas. They'd already killed him when he stood up in the square that day. Now – what do you see, when you look at Abu Firas?

By this point, ABU AL-TAYYIB *has brought down the body of* ABU FIRAS.

ZAHRA. I see what you're telling me.

ABU AL-TAYYIB. It was they who committed his suicide. Even if it looks like something else, what does logic say? (*As he covers* ABU FIRAS.) What is truth in a time of war? What is it? It is a series of little white lies… Made-up stories… That's all.

ZAHRA. It was hard for him to go on living… (*Flustered, she leaves the sentence hanging.*)

ABU AL-TAYYIB. Go on, go on. Don't worry. You are doing great.

ZAHRA *remains silent, shocked.*

You know why Abu Karim was removed from his position?

ZAHRA *doesn't know.*

I will not hide anything from you, comrade. All it takes is money. A weak man like Abu Karim, he opens doors when he should keep them closed.

ZAHRA. I don't follow.

ABU AL-TAYYIB. The leadership doesn't give anyone special treatment.

ABU AL-TAYYIB *is going through* ABU FIRAS*'s pockets. He finds lots of clippings of paper.*

Abu Firas had the luxury of being able to think. And say anything that came into his head.

ABU AL-TAYYIB *takes out a radio from* ABU FIRAS*'s pocket. He turns it on. There is a news item: 'A Scud missile has struck the northern part of the village of al-Buhayrat, inflicting a huge loss of life and damaging buildings. We are waiting for further reports to confirm the full extent of the destruction. Our correspondent in – ' The sound fades into static and then the radio stops working altogether.*

(*Looking at* ABU FIRAS.) The radio has died. How is that for a coincidence! (*Pause.*) Believe it or not, I was fond of Abu Firas. There was something kind about him. And his father, God rest his soul – without him, I would be nothing. He took me by the hand, showed me the way. Maybe that is why I despise him. (*Pause.*) What do you think?

ZAHRA. They should have arrested him, for his own protection.

ABU AL-TAYYIB. Poor man. He thought he had the truth, but all he had was some other fantasy. Everyone lies. People always choose the lies they know, the lies they were brought up on. The lies that they can always believe. It is good he made the decision for himself, the smartest thing he ever did. Don't you think?

ZAHRA *nods in agreement.*

Are you lying?

ZAHRA *is confused, and scared of* ABU AL-TAYYIB.

ZAHRA. I'm not, I swear.

ABU AL-TAYYIB. Do you know what I mean by 'lying'?

ZAHRA. I wanted to ask… What lie?

ABU AL-TAYYIB. What lie?

ZAHRA *remains silent.*

Whether you lie or not, only one thing matters. That what you say is believable. Make no mistakes!

ABU AL-TAYYIB *takes the goat by the neck as if he is about to kill it.* ZAHRA *starts in horror and covers her eyes.*

Surely, you don't think I could kill the thing. Comrade, have you forgotten? I am here to protect the village. (*Lets go of the goat.*) I do my best, and I never get thanked for it. We have to be ruled by the whip, otherwise we all eat each other.

ABU AL-TAYYIB *moves closer to* ZAHRA *in a menacing way, and stands in front of her.*

ZAHRA. Comrade… Martyrdom is not a lie. The war is not a lie. Soon, when it ends –

He stands right in front of her, in a way that flusters her.

ABU AL-TAYYIB. The war is not going to end.

ZAHRA (*confused and scared, bursting into tears*). What's going to happen?

ABU AL-TAYYIB. Zahra, don't be scared. For yourself or for your baby. You are the future of this country. We are going to bury him. Let your students talk. Listen to them. You are there for them. Like I am here for you. Let them say what they feel, and help them see what they should believe. This is a moment to make them soldiers, or deserters. (*Pause.*) Don't forget – get them to write a tribute to their teacher, for the memorial. That is the proper thing, is it not?

ZAHRA *cries.* ABU AL-TAYYIB *embraces her in a fatherly manner.*

I know this is terribly hard for you. He was your teacher. He taught us all. But life is easier this way. Life is possible. When a single stone is knocked out of place, the whole lot tumbles down, like dominoes. I am here to protect you, and to protect all the children of the village.

ZAHRA *cries harder. He gently holds her away and smiles at her.*

If only we'd been born somewhere else.

ZAHRA *leaves, mesmerised.*

ABU AL-TAYYIB *remains with* ABU FIRAS*'s body and the goat. He sits down on one of the classroom chairs, looks around, and thinks.*

Scene Eighteen – Nature

*The cemetery. Daytime. Goats browse among the graves and eat
the wilted flowers left behind.* ABU FIRAS*'s funeral procession
approaches, led by four* MEN *carrying the coffin, which bears
an old photo of* ABU FIRAS. *Behind them is an impressive
parade of* SECURITY MEN *and* OFFICERS *in their various
uniforms, wearing sunglasses, and tracksuits.* BODYGUARDS
clear the path for them.

All the VILLAGERS *are in attendance, plus* ABU FIRAS*'s
family.* IMM AL-TAYYIB *has no hair and wears a kerchief
around her head to cover her burns.* IMM GHASSAN *is
present, and* ZAHRA, *who watches* ABU AL-TAYYIB. *The*
TEENAGERS *are sad and awkward, but they behave well during
the ceremony.* SAMI *checks his mobile whenever he gets the
chance. The coffin is placed on the ground.* ABU AL-TAYYIB *is
clean-shaven, but burn marks are still visible. He makes his way
forward and timidly begins his speech.*

ABU AL-TAYYIB. My dear friends and comrades. Bright
    torches are being extinguished. Soaring eagles of intellect
    are being led to their death. Enlightened minds are killed,
    and our country is ravaged, day after day. Yet – by God – we
    are as determined as ever. Abu Firas comes from an
    honourable family known for its patriotic feeling. He loved
    his family, he loved his nation, and he made a great sacrifice
    for it. As a tribute to our beloved teacher, the authorities are
    converting Abu Firas's home into a school for memorising
    the Qur'an. (*Pause.*) Now, let us pay tribute to our dear
    departed. We have many eulogies. Dr Samer Abu Samra, for
    the Party. Nasim Sulayman, Honourable Minister for
    Education. Ms Lamya Fadhan, for the Peoples' Associations.
    My son Mudar will read the tribute by his pupils. Abu Firas's
    brother, just arrived from abroad, will deliver a eulogy from
    the family. First, Imm Ghassan will speak, for his friends.

They wait expectantly for IMM GHASSAN *to stir, but she
does not move.* ZAHRA *watches her.* IMM GHASSAN
gazes at ABU FIRAS*'s coffin, deep in grief.*

Imm Ghassan, our anguish is great. We await your words to bring us some solace.

Pause. IMM GHASSAN *takes a piece of paper from inside her clothes.*

IMM GHASSAN. If Abu Firas hadn't left his will at my window, if he hadn't wanted it to be read out to you, I would never speak up. This has happened before and nothing changed. But I am reading this, for his sake. (*Pause.*) Abu Firas was a dear friend. He saved a life, the life most dear to me. Abu Firas paid for this will with his life. Those killed by traitors, well, they have no time to leave a will. (*Pause.*) But Abu Firas did leave a will. Here are Abu Firas's final words:

'My poor fellow villagers. Your children call you, they seek your help. When you answer know that you are killing your own children. I asked the question and could not bear the answer. The price I pay is my life. I opened my son's coffin so I could lay down next to him. Now you see my coffin, and you know how Abu Firas died. For you, there is no longer an excuse…'

As IMM GHASSAN *is reading, hail begins to pour down, preventing us from hearing her final words.* IMM AL-TAYYIB *laughs hysterically. The goats delve deeper, trying to dig up the contents of the graves.*

'A great published script makes you understand what the play is, at its heart' *Slate Magazine*

Enjoyed this book? Choose from hundreds more classic and contemporary plays from Nick Hern Books, the UK's leading independent theatre publisher.

Our full range is available to browse online now, including:

Award-winning plays from leading contemporary dramatists, including *King Charles III* by Mike Bartlett, *Anne Boleyn* by Howard Brenton, *Jerusalem* by Jez Butterworth, *A Breakfast of Eels* by Robert Holman, *Chimerica* by Lucy Kirkwood, *The Night Alive* by Conor McPherson, *The James Plays* by Rona Munro, *Nell Gwynn* by Jessica Swale, and many more...

Ground-breaking drama from the most exciting up-and-coming playwrights, including Vivienne Franzmann, James Fritz, Ella Hickson, Anna Jordan, Jack Thorne, Phoebe Waller-Bridge, Tom Wells, and many more...

Twentieth-century classics, including *Cloud Nine* by Caryl Churchill, *Death and the Maiden* by Ariel Dorfman, *Pentecost* by David Edgar, *Angels in America* by Tony Kushner, *Long Day's Journey into Night* by Eugene O'Neill, *The Deep Blue Sea* by Terence Rattigan, *Machinal* by Sophie Treadwell, and many more...

Timeless masterpieces from playwrights throughout the ages, including Anton Chekhov, Euripides, Henrik Ibsen, Federico García Lorca, Christopher Marlowe, Molière, William Shakespeare, Richard Brinsley Sheridan, Oscar Wilde, and many more...

Every playscript is a world waiting to be explored. Find yours at **www.nickhernbooks.co.uk** – you'll receive a 20% discount, plus free UK postage & packaging for orders over £30.

'Publishing plays gives permanent form to an evanescent art, and allows many more people to have some kind of experience of a play than could ever see it in the theatre' *Nick Hern, publisher*

www.nickhernbooks.co.uk

A Nick Hern Book

Goats was first published in Great Britain in 2017 as a paperback original
by Nick Hern Books Limited, The Glasshouse, 49a Goldhawk Road, London
W12 8QP, in association with the Royal Court Theatre, London

Associate translator: Yasmine Seale

Cover design by Root

Designed and typeset by Nick Hern Books, London
Printed in Great Britain by Ashford Colour Press, Gosport, Hampshire

A CIP catalogue record for this book is available from the British Library

ISBN   978 1 84842 720 4

www.nickhernbooks.co.uk

facebook.com/nickhernbooks

twitter.com/nickhernbooks